90

MORE DAYS
WITH
JESUS

90 MORE DAYS WITH JESUS

A GUIDE FOR GROWTH

BRAD OLSEN

ILLUMIFY

MEDIA.COM

90 More Days with Jesus
Copyright © 2024 by Brad Olsen

The views and opinions expressed in this book are those of the author and
do not necessarily reflect the official policy or position of
Illumify Media Global.

Published by
Revolworks Publishing
Illumify Media Global
www.IllumifyMedia.com
"Let's bring your book to life!"

Paperback ISBN: 978-1-955043-84-7

Typeset by Art Innovations (http://artinnovations.in/)
Cover design by Debbie Lewis

Printed in the United States of America

CONTENTS

INTRODUCTION

How would you organize the best material to cause its readers to grow spiritually? Such was the goal of a small group of writers twenty years ago. A group of talented interns learning to be spiritual leaders set out to create a devotional that would lend itself to applying Jesus' most important teachings from the Scriptures.

I cherry-picked five of the best writers from our postgraduate internship program: Adam Boyd, Amy Laughlin Williams, Karen Simmons, Hollis Barth, and Liz Doescher. The goal was to create a book that would distill some of Jesus' most profound teachings and describe them on a single page.

We started with a devotional title, followed by a clever quote and three Scripture passages. Those were followed by a page of commentary and concluded with engaging discussion questions.

We wrote extensively through several years to create this guide. We tested the devotionals on our website revolworks. com. Over time, we massaged the writings and paired them down to 180 of the best ones.

Through that effort we came up with two volumes of 90 devotionals each. This is the second volume. Whether used as a guide for a small group or a daily devotional, these thoughts should transform your understanding of Jesus and his favorite topics. Looking back through history, we realize that there are relatively few great leaders, and none of them live up to the life, teachings, and leadership of Jesus of Nazareth.

Feel free to use this guide as a daily devotional or as a weekly outline for your group. Either way, we hope and pray that you will be challenged and encouraged.

UNITY

NOT MY WILL

"God's plan for your life is happening right now.
It doesn't begin when you get married or when you get
your dream job or when everything feels perfect.
You are in the plan."

— TARA LEIGH COBBLE

| Matthew 6:9-13 | Matthew 26:36-46 | 1 John 2:16-17 |

The concept of "God's will" was the hot topic of spiritual writers in the mid-1980s. It seemed everyone had a definition of what God's will meant, but few felt satisfactory.

With the right definition, we thought, God's will would make sense. Trusting it would be natural. Yet such a complete trust remained, and remains, elusive. We spend more time ensuring that God has a substantial to-do list, so He doesn't mess with us too much.

The Lord's Prayer says, "Thy Kingdom come, Thy will be done." We have said these lines more often than we can count. But do we really trust God and His will? It comes down to control. Are we willing to give it up or not?

The Scriptures are filled with descriptions of God's plans for us, how good they are, how pleasant and profitable. Yet we still don't trust Him. He's too much of a meddler.

One line is often repeated by my friend Marty: "God wants more for you than you want for yourself." Just as we give a financial advisor control over our assets, we can depend on God to manage our biggest investment, our life, better than we can imagine.

If He really wants more for us than we do, we should probably give Him more leeway. We've heard the Lord's Prayer often, yet we have a problem with one of its most basic tenets. We still struggle with God's call to release our to-do list and fall into the better plan that He has for us.

Never was Jesus more relatable in His humanity than in Gethsemane. He struggled with the pain that was bearing down on Him. He sweat blood. He asked God to take the suffering away. He surrendered His will: "Not My will, but Thine."

Periods of pain in life are inevitable. Chronic illness, loss, and trauma bring ongoing trials. Yet somehow the Lord grants us the faith to believe that He wants more for us than we want for ourselves.

Brad

▫ **What events have caused you to tighten the grip on your life?**

▫ **What stands in the way of releasing your life to God's will?**

▫ **What does this release look like?**

ORDERLY MYSTERY

Jerry Landers: If you're God,
how can You permit all the suffering
that goes on in the world?
God: I don't permit the suffering – you do.

— OH GOD! (1977)

Genesis 1	John 1:1-5	Matthew 15:12-20

Creationists chortle: "God created everything!"
Who then created evil?

Such questions stump experts and baffle the mind. We see a world created with astounding order. Organisms heal themselves, animals procreate, cells divide, DNA patterns predict life, food chains maintain balance, seasons change in predictable cycles, the sun rises every day, the moon revolves, the earth rotates, universes exist in seamless order.

We view this all from the most perfect observation platform: the earth's surface. It is as if the Creator wanted to impress us. Case in point: our sun is 400 times the size of our moon. The sun also lies 400 times the distance from earth's surface. . . so we can predictably view a perfect solar eclipse. Scientists will tell you that, because the moon blocks the sun's light, they have made monumental discoveries about the sun's surface.

Our planet possesses the perfect mixture of gases to provide a transparent atmosphere. Alter the combination slightly, as is the case on other planets, and we would have no view of the heavens. And we would cook.

It would require overwhelming determination to believe any of these natural occurrences were accidental. No, our Creator designed a world full of astounding order and purpose.

It is as if the Great Lover were giving His bride the ultimate view of His kingdom, an immense comfort. Yet other ideas confuse.

Why would a loving and all-powerful god allow pain and suffering?

Why does evil exist?

Why are so many truths incompatible?

While confusing us, these questions also raise the mystery of God. We realize that our intellectual arms are much too short to embrace all truth.

Majestic order and baffling mystery. Would you want your god to be any other way?

Brad

———◆———

❏ **How have you observed natural order?**

❏ **What mysteries baffle you most about God?**

❏ **How do you reconcile the two ideas?**

PURPOSE AND PERVERSION

"You possess a potent force that you either use,
or misuse, hundreds of times every day."

— J. MARTIN KOHE

| Genesis 1, 2 | John 1:1-14 | Romans 2:1-11 |

Inventors create products with a purpose in mind. Alexander Graham Bell created the telephone for long-distance communication. Wilbur and Orville Wright invented the airplane for advanced transportation. The makers of Sudafed developed pseudoephedrine to relieve cold and flu symptoms. And Philo Farnsworth invented the television to allow people around the world to learn about each other in the hopes of settling differences around a conference table instead of the battlefields of world wars.

Over time we've seen these purposes perverted. Telemarketers harass their subjects over the phone. Terrorists hijack airplanes and turn them into deadly missiles. Broadcast media polarize viewers by highlighting division and presenting greedy and sexually exploitative cultural norms. Addicts cook pseudoephedrine to make methamphetamine.

The great Architect of the universe created our home planet with a good purpose in mind. When Moses wrote the first chapter of Genesis, he punctuated one point. "In the beginning God created the heavens and the earth . . . and God saw that it was good." (Genesis 1:1, 10)

He repeats the goodness of creation in verses 4, 12, 18, 21, 25, and 31. His point: every created thing possesses a good purpose. Yet each one also carries a similar and proportionate capacity for perversion. No created thing is morally neutral.

Whatever you can imagine was created through Jesus according to Scripture (John 1:3). And He created it with a good purpose. Make your own list: animals, trees, the ocean, people, emotions (yes, even anger), money, sex. Each of these possess a divine purpose for good.

So how does bad happen? When we pervert the purpose. The devil has no creative powers, but he can lead astray. God created sex to satisfy our longing for intimacy in marriage. Utilize this gift in marriage, God says, and it will bless us. Use it outside of marriage, and we are cursed.

As we weigh various purposes, we see a litmus test for life. Am I using this thing for its created purpose? Why am I finding myself in this situation? Lord, what do you want to teach me here? We need to ask ourselves these questions, then try to decipher the Lord's purpose. When we discover it, we should follow that path with tenacity no matter the cost.

Brad

- **What in creation have you used for good? How?**

- **What in creation have you perverted? How?**

- **What were the outcomes?**

LIFE FROM DEATH

"Call me morbid, but I love funerals.
They teach me about life."

— ANONYMOUS

| Matthew 25:31-46 | Job 3 | Ecclesiastes 1 |

What's my favorite eulogy? you ask. Gregg Kremer portrayed the best quality in his father, Ken. Already wise in his mid-twenties, Gregg approached the microphone. He bore all the markings of a Nebraska farmer: deeply tanned forearms, snowy white forehead, rough hands, and a slight drawl.

Returning from missionary duties in Korea, Gregg's father and mother, Ken and Lila, settled in Aurora, Nebraska, to raise their children on the family farm. They wanted to instill strong Midwestern values in their children while surrounded by members of Ken's family in a small farming community. His father, Maurice, made his name as a highly regarded state senator. He was a man of few words, yet Nebraskans remember his sharp observations, keen wit, and trustworthy pledges.

But back to Gregg. I smiled to myself as he began to speak. Ken and Lila would have done the same at the way he expressed himself: simple, profound, humble.

"The thing about my dad," he said, "is that he'd show up."

"It seems that whenever me or the other kids had problems, Dad showed up. When we heard rumors that a couple was having marriage problems, Dad showed up. When someone was sick or in the hospital, Dad showed up. When a new neighbor moved to town, Dad showed up."

Wow!

He figured it out. In the end, it's not about reaching the pinnacle of a career, nor living in a beautiful house, nor driving the right car, nor the number of zeros in one's net worth, nor the size of the city where one lives, nor the titles after a name, nor the heights of one's fame.

People don't talk about those topics at funerals.

They will, however, remember the small acts of kindness. "I was hungry, and he gave me something to eat. I was thirsty, and she gave me something to drink. I was a stranger, and he invited me in. I was naked, and she clothed me. I was sick, and he comforted me. I was in prison, and he visited me."

As mourners ponder the life of the deceased, they either bless or curse the memories. Few things are sadder than a misspent life.

It's our choice. People will remember us for extending the little graces. Or our legacies become defined by the pain we caused others.

Brad

———— ✦ ————

- Do *you* focus on *yourself* and *your* agendas or the needs of others?

- Who is someone for whom you have high regard? Why?

- How do you want to be remembered?

BUSY

"It is difficult not to have plans, not to organize people around an urgent cause, and not to feel that you are working directly for social progress. But I wonder more and more if the first thing shouldn't be to know people by name, to eat and drink with them, to listen to their stories and tell your own, and to let them know with words, handshakes, and hugs that you do not simply like them, but you truly love them."

— HENRI NOUWEN

Ecclesiastes 2:10-11	Matthew 7:21-23	1 John 4:7-12

Modern Americans typically keep a calendar of their daily, weekly, and monthly activities. We create lists, make appointments, and schedule lunches. Whether the list is handwritten or exists on a cellphone, the truth remains the same—our calendar drives our daily lives.

Perhaps our busy schedules explain why we don't ponder our purpose. Because at the end of a day, we can point to meetings, events, and people that filled our time slots.

Jesus cares about our calendars and how we spend our time. Not just now, not just for us, but for Him and for eternity. One of the most terrifying truths Jesus tells his disciples is, "Not everyone who says to Me, 'Lord, Lord,' will enter the kingdom of heaven" (Matthew 7:21). Something more than recognition of Jesus as Lord is required of us. Our faith needs wheels and an engine.

Jesus focuses more on the heart than the action. More than this, Jesus says that "he who does the will of My Father who is in heaven" will enter the kingdom of heaven.

Believers today presume much regarding the Lord's work. Christians often lean toward serving the poor, visiting impoverished nations, and being missionaries in foreign lands because these are actions of the saints. But if the emphasis is on the heart, the greatest work yet may be to learn the art of solitude.

Jesus didn't rush hither and yon. His life required no scheduler. Jesus spent His time walking place to place, speaking to the people who crossed his path, and loving them.

When the Pharisees asked Jesus how they should live, he left the options wide open. He said, "Love the Lord your God with all your heart and with all your soul and with all your mind" and "love your neighbor as yourself" (Matthew 22:37, 39).

Without giving specifications, Jesus directed that these two commandments should dictate how we spend our days. We can have our meetings, plan our lunches, and fill our schedules, but in the midst of it all, we need to care for people and pursue the Father. If we focus on the first part but find ourselves neglecting the second, then perhaps we need to slow down and ask our Father what He would have us do.

Brad

———◆———

- When you look at your calendar, how do you see your time being spent?

- To what extent do these activities match your desired purpose for life?

- What needs to change?

BEGINNINGS

"A man can endure any what
as long as he knows the why."

— VIKTOR FRANKL,
MAN'S SEARCH FOR MEANING

Philippians 3:7-11	Micah 6:8	1 Thessalonians 5:16-22

My sophomore year of college I enrolled in linear algebra, an ominous but necessary class to fulfill my intended math major.

Two years later, I graduated with a degree in Spanish and Economics. The linear algebra helped me make the change. Regardless, I remember the class. The three-hour exams that consisted of only two problems. The endless computations utilizing theorems, equations, and rules. The indescribable sense of victory that I extracted from completing just one of these questions. Looking at a graded test with utter disappointment when three pages of correctly executed equations led to an incorrect solution. I started with the wrong initial value.

Purpose is where we begin. It serves as the initial value that guides the equations of our lives. It imparts meaning and significance. It is the basis, the value in lowest terms, the origin of significance. It exists as a mystery in its simplicity, so simple to state yet so much more complex to live.

We can state the how, but we continually strive to decipher the why. The why exists as the journey, and as Homer acknowledged, "The journey is the thing." Knowing true purpose serves as the solid base from which to pursue life, a skewed knowledge of this leads only to further misdirection. It is futile to pursue the right actions for the wrong reasons and the wrong actions for the right reasons.

What is our purpose?

The obvious, easily packaged purpose: to love the Lord with all your heart, soul, mind, and strength. Yet the mysterious question of how persists. We embark on a lifelong journey with this acceptance of paradox. Do we abandon the journey when the pathway seems shrouded and the direction dark and dim? Or do we trust? Wendell Berry challenged us to "ask the questions that have no answers."

We didn't attempt calculus or linear algebra when we entered elementary school. We learned addition. And then subtraction, followed by multiplication, division, fractions, and so on. Our ability grows as our knowledge increases.

Our understanding of purpose reveals itself in broader scope as we live life and love the Lord. If we derive our purpose from the Lord and devote ourselves to living in and for His love, the how of purpose reveals itself.

Amy

———— ◆ ————

▢   **What is the basis of your knowledge of purpose?**

▢   **How do you react to the unknown in your life?**

▢   **What is your purpose?**

DAY 7

PERFECTION

"Being perfect is... about you and your relationship
with yourself, your family and your friends.
Being perfect is about being able to look your friends
in the eye and know that you didn't let them down
because you told them the truth."

— COACH GARY GAINES
IN THE MOVIE, FRIDAY NIGHT LIGHTS

| 1 Peter 1:15-16 | Leviticus 11:44-45 | Leviticus 19:1-4 |

Despite our widespread and deep-seated notions of perfection, it is not what we think. We look at perfection as something involving a great veneer—don't smoke, curse, drink, wear baggy clothes, see R-rated movies, sleep late, or spend too much money.

Jesus never defined perfection by adhering to these rules. He emphasized loving enemies, turning evil on its head by responding with love, honoring marriage, and reconciling with debtors. Jesus viewed life, and the perfection of it, in entirely relational terms.

This is an important distinction to grasp. In our world, perfection denotes a degree of achievement or performance as measured by and against others. But Jesus understood perfection more fully and more clearly: it isn't just about some performance in competition with others, but in our relating with others.

To borrow from a political phrase, It's the people, stupid. How do we treat them? How do we serve them? How do we consider them above ourselves? How do we dispense mercy, kindness, gratitude, generosity, grace? Do we live for others, especially the Lord?

You see, we can't just live any way we choose, because we matter to God. Therefore, we must matter to one another, because through this, God shows us that He loves us and wants something better for us than our short-sighted self-indulgence; that's a reckless way of living that not only neglects the needs of others, but also endangers them.

Other people matter. God loves people and wants us to love them too. He wants us to give to them, to look out for their best interests ahead of our own. This is the road to perfection.

We've gone about this morality business all wrong, missing all the points the Scriptures make. Profanity, alcohol, television violence, and premarital sex were never Jesus issues with us. They are the issues we had among ourselves. They are the symptoms we focus on to the exclusion of the real illness.

Jesus was concerned with the underlying problem and its more specific manifestations: cursing our neighbors; drinking to escape others while creating more relational hazards; kneeling before an altar of violence; sex in such a way that it causes us to lose our inherent value. All these acts indicate deeper issues in the heart and stem from them.

A life free of tobacco, alcohol, profanity and sex does not lead to holiness or perfection. Devoid of love, all it creates is an alienating facade that lies about the truth and screams deceitfully about perfection. We must understand His teachings and to whom they point. Until we get this, we'll miss what Jesus wants us to learn. As long as we focus our attention and energies on peripheral issues, we'll miss it. And if we do that, we'll miss the kingdom itself.

Adam

☐ **What is perfection? Holiness?**

☐ **How do we understand them?**

☐ **What do they imply about us, our lives?**

WHITHER PURPOSE?

"It is not enough to be busy. So are the ants. The question is: What are we busy about?"

— HENRY DAVID THOREAU

| Luke 10:25-37 | Philippians 4:8-9 | 2 Chronicles 17:3-6 |

Howard Schultz's vision had two purposes: create a great work environment and produce "the best coffee experience possible." Starbucks was born. *Jerry Maguire* centered on a sports agent struggling with his own purpose and direction in a life that screamed, "Show me the money!" Rick Warren's *Purpose-Driven Life* has sold more than 30 million copies, shattering records at every turn. Best-seller lists, song lyrics, institutional mission statements, and movies all indicate that we increasingly think about this idea of purpose. What is our purpose?

Perhaps we've allowed this question to lapse for too long. Well-established traditions, cultural patterns, and social routines make us think we've answered this question. To ask it again is unnecessary at best and irresponsible when doing so demands any of our time. Life's expected duties:—school, work, family, success—await.

Yet why do we engage in these activities? What stirs us to rise each morning, take up our to-do lists, and begin checking off tasks? And who or what determines the list? Despite our subtle misgivings in this routine, at least we take comfort standing in the same line as everyone else. To ask the question might compel us to step out of line, that one place where we find comfort. Better not risk losing that, in addition to certainty. Still, we wonder what makes for real life, what it's all about.

Luke's expert in the law asked Jesus what He should do to really live. To everyone's dismay, Jesus didn't prescribe a list of activities: where to work, how to spend His money, for whom to vote, or where to worship. However, He did offer a few words enormous in their simplicity. Sort of like Curly's one thing in *City Slickers*. It feels so esoteric and Zen-like in its simplicity.

Jesus said love is the one thing. With all passions and commitment, all desires and efforts, all thoughts and will, love the Lord. Love others with the same devotion you show yourself. That's all.

We so often believe we need to work certain jobs to win God's favor or to live like the spiritual giants of yesteryear. Yet when Jesus explained what makes for real life, he said otherwise.

He kept it simple and told us to think about these two things: love God and love each other. This is what you need remember, and it'll be enough for this moment, this hour, this day, this life. To do so will consume all of your resources. It'll probably prove too much for you, but that's good. Because you'll find in loving that you forget everything but the other person, even God. That's life."

□   **What is your purpose in your family life? In your work? In your faith?**

□   **What do you tell others your purpose is?**

□   **What do you tell yourself your purpose is?**

DAY 9

MOUNTAINS

"The journey is the thing."

— HOMER

| Luke 5:17-28 | Joshua 1:1-9 | Genesis 12:1-5 |

We crave the ultimate finale, an accomplished finish line, a terminus. Yet when adopting the Lord's purpose as our own, we must abandon this desire. We must exchange it instead for a lifelong pursuit of something not fully knowable.

We may answer the question, What is your purpose in life? with love God, love others. But it takes a lifetime to put into practice. How do I love the Lord today? This afternoon? This hour? This minute?

And we grow. We age. Our capacities to understand increase. We grow into purpose as we grow into our awkwardly large feet and oversized childhood ears. We understand in retrospect not in foresight.

I remember childhood winters in Michigan: long, lazy days that glow in my memory like the brilliant white sunlit snow. I remember climbing what seemed Everest-like heights to reach the sledding hill's apex, and the fearful prospect of embarking on a surely death-defying trip down.

My palms sweated in my thermal mittens, and I could feel my heart anxiously pounding, even though it was buried under twelve layers of winter clothing. I lay on the sled, pushed off, and flew down the icy slope. In my mind it was steeper than straight down. I was breaking the sound barrier. The trip, although short, lasted long enough. I escaped with my life.

A few years ago, I returned to that same spot, excited to once again stand in awe of the lofty greatness of the "mountain."

"There it is," my mom motioned to what barely resembled a small hill.

"Where?" I responded, indignant that this paltry rise was the same slope on which I risked my life. But as she motioned again to the same place, I understood. I outgrew this hill. I outgrew this challenge. My strength was greater, my knowledge deeper, and my courage fiercer.

I still climb. I climb higher, attempting to summit Rocky Mountain peaks.

As the Haitian proverb states, "Beyond [those] mountains there are mountains."

Beyond those challenges rise more difficult challenges. The summit is not the final goal. The purpose lies in the journey not the destination. The now is the thing: the now, the current striving of our hearts. We must endeavor farther up and farther into our own lives, into that beautiful, mysterious, and vast inner topography of our hearts.

Greater challenges. Deeper revelations. Growing. Outgrowing. Learning.

In I Corinthians Paul realizes, "For now we see in a mirror dimly, but then face to face; now I know in part, then I will know fully just as I also have been fully known" (13:12).

Then we shall know fully. Now we strive continually toward Jesus and His purpose.

Amy

———◆———

◻ **How much bigger is God's purpose than your own?**

◻ **What are you struggling with now?**

◻ **How does it feel to be on the peak? In the valley?**

DAY 10

WHY DID YOUR PARENTS WANT YOU?

"The grace of God means something like:
Here is your life. You might never have been,
but you are because the party wouldn't have been
complete without you."

— FREDERICK BUECHNER

| Genesis 2:18-25 | Jeremiah 31:3 | Psalm 139:13 |

For some children, the question Why did your parents want you? may hurt too much to ask. The answers don't always fill us with a sense of belonging. Words like *mistake*, *accident*, and *unplanned* hang over some lives. "You weren't in the cards." "We didn't expect you." "I didn't ask for you. And now you are here."

A young, first-grade teacher, hoping to illustrate the deeper meaning, once asked her students this question. The answers came quickly: "To take out the trash." "To help with chores." "My parents say tax credit and laugh whenever I ask them."

Finally, one child replied, "Because they loved me."

Sadly, parents overcook the importance of chores or tax credits. Others simply fail to communicate the unsophisticated truth: "I wanted you. That's why you are here."

Children, whether young or in middle age, wake each morning without knowing that their life happened on purpose. They don't realize fully that someone willed them into being.

A young couple recently mentioned their desire to have a child. They enjoy a lovely marriage, many friends, and a great life for twenty-somethings. Yet they feel something is missing, something only a child can provide. The love between them is not inadequate; the love stimulates the desire to procreate.

The strong desire to be wanted dramatically alters the way we see life. The questions to which we wake up differ. No longer do we ask, "Why am I here?" Rather, we ask, "How do I live my life, and what do I do with it?" A deep understanding of another's love affects such change.

A few minutes' conversation with small children demonstrates this principle. Notice the ones who believe they're loved and are wanted by their parents. Then look at those who aren't. The buoyancy and liveliness of the former forecast their lives.

American theologian Frederick Buechner read a sermon once. In it God awoke one day, looked around, and said, "I'm lonely. I think I'll make me a world." God then made man to be with Him. Just as Adam's world felt incomplete without Eve, so God felt His world incomplete without us. Not just the collective us but every individual. Jesus' parable of the lost sheep in Luke chapter 15 speaks of each person's inestimable worth: the shepherd would leave ninety-nine to search out the lost one.

Hearing this, we still reach to believe that we matter. Though we hear it from parents, friends, or spouses—though Jesus tells us—we doubt. Thus, the work of God is and ever will be to believe. We must live like we believe we are wanted, knowing that the world is incomplete without each of us.

New questions wait. "How do I live my life, and what do I do with it?"

Adam

———◆———

☐   **Are you here on purpose or for a purpose?**

☐   **To what extent do you believe that someone, God or your parents, wanted you to be here right now?**

☐   **If you were created to be God's friend, how does this affect your daily life?**

WHO AM I?

"What deadens us most to God's presence within us,
I think, is the inner dialogue that we are
continuously engaged with ourselves,
the endless chatter of human thought."

— FREDERICK BUECHNER

Mark 1:9	Psalm 139	Romans 8:28-39

Hundreds of years ago a Roman centurion approached a rabbi on the street, cornering him with two questions: Who are you? and Where are you going?

"How much money do you make?" responded the rabbi.

Taken aback, the soldier responded with some normal sum. The rabbi offered to double the soldier's income if he would stand outside his door and ask him those questions every day.

Who am I? Where am I going? And where do I seek the answers to those questions? Do I strive to find the answers in accomplishments? In academics? In performance? In family, friends, and popularity? In approval? To whose accolades and applause do I turn my ear? To whose recognition do I respond?

Who am I, and where am I going? Am I just a lemming? A follower of some elusive pied piper? Blindly and mindlessly following someone unknown? Am I adhering more to the words of some musician saying, "I don't know where I'm going, but I'm getting there fast?"

For all my self-awareness and self-perception, do I continue following that elusive drumbeat? Is it more automation than autonomy? Do I run as fast as I can regardless of the destination?

Flannery O'Conner stated, "Somewhere is better than anywhere." Where is my somewhere, and why am I going there?

We seldom recognize the misguided pursuits of our lives. Yet they appear obvious at a distance. Dogs, those creatures heralded as man's best friend, illustrate the fickle dependency of our responses. We stroke their heads, pat their fur, and they sit contently, appeased. We move our hand. The dog, desperately seeking the same approval, also moves. The process continues. Dogs are approval junkies. So are we. Where do I find my strokes?

I find approval and contentment in accomplishments, pursuits, academics, performance, family, friends, and numerous relationships. I can find it in these places, but I will ultimately find myself unfulfilled and deceived. Humans will fail me; endeavors will prove unsuccessful; accomplishments won't satisfy, and my own performance will continue to require greater achievement. These entities exist only as imitations and substitutes, paltry replacements for the real.

The reality is that I am God's child. Just as God proclaimed after Jesus' baptism, "This is My Son with whom I am well pleased," God proclaims that about us daily.

This is my son. My daughter.
With whom I am well pleased.
If only we could better listen.

Amy

————◆————

- ☐ **If you could hear God's proclamation and believe it, how would your life change?**

- ☐ **If it were only His voice that you listened to, who would you say He is?**

- ☐ **Where would you say He is going?**

DAY 12

THOUGHTS ON PERFECTION

"Love never ends. As for prophecies,
they will pass away; as for tongues, they will cease;
as for knowledge, it will pass away. For we know in part,
and we prophesy in part, but when the perfect comes,
the partial will pass away."

— 1 CORINTHIANS 13:8-10 ESV

1Corinthians 13:1-3	1Corinthians 13:4-7	1 Corinthians 13:8-13

Perfection is a prison. We start out reaching for good, but we end up in bondage. The perfection we seek is an illusion. But when the *perfect One comes again*, the partial things will fade away.

I have strived for perfection my whole life. I know personally how much of a prison this pursuit can become. Unfortunately, I've also expected the same of my wife and kids. In doing so, I inevitably set them up for failure because perfection is unattainable. Instead of helping them, I damage my relationship with them. I'm grateful that the Lord has helped them mostly recover from my many mistakes.

The Scriptures speak of perfection in the Old Testament in a very specific context: the Law. For example, Psalm 19:7 says, "The Law of the LORD is perfect, restoring the soul." Seldom do the Scriptures talk about a person being perfect. Rather, the New Testament talks about how wonderfully imperfect we are. The Sermon on the Mount (Matthew 5-7) especially highlights the fact that the Lord fully loves and embraces us despite our imperfection.

For example, rather than blessing those who uphold the law perfectly, Jesus says, "Blessed are the poor in spirit, for theirs is the kingdom of heaven."

There are three words used for *poor* in Greek, each denoting a certain degree of poverty. The word used in this occasion refers to the most poverty-stricken level or the poorest of the poor. It refers to a person forced to beg for everything. Instead of rebuking or cursing these people, He calls them blessed.

He takes the people who must beg and places them over His kingdom. It's an amazing insight to understand. It's a countercultural phenomenon. Rather than appointing the best of the best over His kingdom, He promotes the weakest people with nothing to give. It's His joy to bless them.

When we strive for perfection, it's almost like deciding, "I'm not going to go out to these social occasions unless my hair is perfect. I mean not even one hair out of place!" Of course, this thinking is ridiculous. It prevents us from enjoying fullness of life and fullness of relationships. We can never be perfect by earthly or cultural standards. Yet Jesus says, "You are to be perfect as the heavenly Father is perfect" (Matthew 5:48). Does this mean we fall short?

No, Jesus is saying that we are to be perfect because He is making us perfect in His image—not here and now but on a spiritual level, in the eternal. This is a process. And when Perfection Himself finally does come, our partial imperfections will be done away.

Brad

———◆———

◻ **To what extent do you place *perfect* expectations on yourself, your family, and others?**

◻ **How does knowing that you are imperfect affect your relationship with God?**

◻ **Does this knowledge drive you away from Him or toward Him?**

HORIZONTAL UNITY

"The overall purpose of human communication is—or should be—reconciliation. It should ultimately serve to lower or remove the walls of misunderstanding which unduly separate us human beings, one from another."

— M. SCOTT PECK

| Matthew 5:23-26 | Hebrews 12:14 | John 16:7-11 |

Brian was the quintessential strait-laced, Midwestern fraternity boy: funny, nerdy, and leader of a well-attended Bible study. His position endeared him to most students but made him a nuisance to others. Some in the fraternity were skeptical of his influence and feared that the house's reputation would decline as the Bible thumping went up. As the year wore on, tension with one critic became apparent. Brian sensed that Chris had developed disdain for him and remembered Jesus' admonishment in the book of Matthew: "Therefore, if you are offering your gift at the altar and there remember that your brother or sister has something against you, leave your gift there in front of the altar. First go and be reconciled to them; then come and offer your gift" (Matthew 5:23-24).

I really don't have anything to be sorry about, thought Brian one night as he went to bed. But he couldn't shake Chris' aversion from his mind. Midnight rolled around, and soon it was one o'clock, and he still couldn't sleep. It appeared that the Holy Spirit was preventing his slumber.

Okay, God, fine. I'll call him and get this over with. But it's gonna be your fault when this ticks him off, he muttered to himself as he rolled out of bed. *There's no way he'll be up... if I call the house phone and nobody answers, then I'm off the hook.* The phone in the hallway rang once, twice, and *Click*

"Hello?"

"Yeah, this is Brian. Chris isn't still up, is he?"

"As a matter of fact, he just walked out of the bathroom."

Brian groaned inwardly.

"Hey, Chris, phone for you." Pause. "Hello?"

"Hey, Chris. It's Brian. I'm calling because I know I've been acting like a self-righteous prig, and I've been lying in bed for two hours trying to convince myself not to call you. I wanted to tell you I'm sorry and see if you'd consider forgiving me."

Something changed on the other end of the line. "You've been lying awake thinking about me? The first day I met you I thought you were a complete hypocrite. Maybe you're not as bad as I thought."

We're called to love God first. We fixate on this noble goal, but we can only accomplish it if we are reconciled with our fellow earth-mates. Jesus places such a premium on the horizontal unity of His followers that He urges us to leave our gifts and go make things right. "Go on, get!" He urges.

How will we know if there's a brother or sister holding a grudge against us, rightfully or not? What if we keep "offering our gift" in futility because we don't recognize the open wound with our name on it?

Thankfully, we're not solely responsible. The Holy Spirit brings a sensitivity that surpasses our own. We don't have to figure out who needs our attention here on earth. We must simply listen and ask to be led.

Hollis

- ☐ **Who came to your mind while reading this?**

- ☐ **What fears do you have about reaching out to this person?**

- ☐ **What promptings might you be ignoring?**

CLEANING UP

"Someday, somebody's going to have to wipe your a—.'

— MORRIE SCHWARTZ, TUESDAYS WITH MORRIE

| 2 Corinthians 12:7-10 | 1 Corinthians 15:42-58 | 2 Corinthians 13:4 |

A friend and I visited his mom in the stroke recovery wing at the hospital. A few days earlier, a stroke impaired her ability to function. We arrived, greeted her, then took her down the hall to the cafeteria for dinner.

Next to me sat an African-American man who shivered as he ate his dinner. I tried to strike up pleasant conversation, but each attempt was met with silence. I realized that a stroke had robbed him of his speech. He responded warmly to each attempt to communicate, especially when I offered him a freshly baked chocolate chip cookie.

Suddenly, he spewed his dinner all over the tray. Not just once but over and over again. His tray and the table were covered with the watery remains of dinner. He simply had no control over his body's convulsing. The staff sprang into action, threw towels over the mess, and whisked the embarrassed Mr. Pinkerton to his room.

My friend looked at his mom. "You know how that feels, don't you?"

Only a few days earlier, she had had the same experience. Her face revealed a sense of deep empathy. Around the dining room, everyone seemed to understand the plight of Mr. Pinkerton. They bore his pain.

It was later explained to me that strokes sometimes paralyze the epiglottis, a floppy valve at the bottom of our throats. The valve separates food and liquids from air. It ably sends solids and liquids into the stomach and gasses into the lungs. Our consciousness pays no attention. Until the process fails.

Mr. Pinkerton's body rejected the food from his lungs to save him from suffocation. The effective result was the humiliating display in the dining hall.

Humiliating but effective. We've all endured humiliation on one level or another, some in the physical realm, some in the emotional, some in the spiritual. And though these moments defy our understanding, others relate to us in the midst of the humiliation, failure, pain, or suffering.

It's odd. We love to see winners. But we can't relate to them. Our own insecurities require a show of pain or humility before we can connect with someone in their soul. When we get such a connection, love and friendship spring up. Vulnerability fertilizes the connection. Bragging smothers it.

We shouldn't walk about as if there's nothing wrong with us. If so, we're wearing a thin façade that can't hide our failures or vices. Sooner or later, we'll need someone to clean up after us. Then Jesus must enter in.

———◆———

- ☐ **When and how have you suffered humiliation?**
- ☐ **Did you tell anyone about it? Why or why not?**
- ☐ **What weaknesses, failures, or embarrassments are you hiding?**

DAY 15

HELP

"Help! I need somebody! Help! Not just anybody!
Won't you please, please help me."

— THE BEATLES

| Ecclesiastes 4:8-12 | Matthew 7:1-6 | Mark 10:46-52 |

We struggle with dependency. We may not need. I won't allow myself to need. We will not ask for help. I would rather be needed than need. I would rather provide than be the one requiring provision.

Last night I sat at dinner with a couple of friends. One friend turned to me and the friend sitting next to me. "I hate saying this, but I need you guys," she said.

You need me? Really? Because I need you too. I don't think you are weak. I don't think you are needy. In you, I see myself. In your need, I feel more comfortable with needing as well.

Earlier that day I watched a man order at a coffee shop. A simple, commonplace event for nearly everyone in the world, except for him. This man was a little person, and even though he was mobile with the help of an electric wheelchair, the extreme shortness of his limbs made even the most basic actions laborious.

While waiting for his coffee he knocked a book off the nearby table. Unable to reach the ground and put it back in place, the man had to tell the barista. As he wheeled to the door, coffee in hand, he had to turn to my friend and me, asking for one of us to open the door.

Two requests for help in the span of merely a few minutes.

Yet, in his inability I saw strength, the strength to know his needs and ask confidently for others to meet them. It cost the barista nothing to reach down and pick up the book. It cost my friend nothing to push open the door. It only cost the man the self-acknowledgement of his own need.

Perhaps he is lucky; his need is obvious. Yet we all need. We are all crippled and undergrown in other areas of our lives. As much as we wish for self-sufficiency, we simply cannot do it. We need our friends to listen to us and observe our lives. We need them to witness the day-to-day struggles and validate our existence. We need others to pick up the figurative books that we drop on the floor and for them to push open the doors that would remain shut due to our inability, both from the shortness of our limbs or from the fullness of the things we carry.

We need God to tell us who we really are because we cannot see ourselves clearly. The world around us just screams lies.

Amy

- How do you need other people?

- Why is it hard for you to ask for help?

- How do other people need you?

DAY 16

COUNTING THE COST

"The old man said, 'You gotta have a good imagination
if you're gonna live the life of old.' He said, 'You've got
to drive that Ford like it's a stallion, and you've got to
wear your heart just like a gun.'"

— JACK INGRAM, "BEAT UP FORD"

| Luke 14:25-33 | Matthew 25:1-13 | Matthew 16:24-28 |

There are two costs. Count them both before you choose.

If you see deep, close-knit friendships that ride out life's storms and selfishness and wounds and fatigue and career, you will surely want one. Something so refined possesses great beauty. But such a beautiful and exquisite thing costs greatly.

If you want it, know this: you will go through rough times. The people you love most will wound you most deeply.

You will be asked to give up what you want. Not every moment but often.

You will be forced to choose often. You will have to choose to know others and let them know you, the real you. It'll terrify you periodically. Visions of betrayals, retreats, abandonment, and exhaustion will pass before your eyes. You risk each.

You will need to lean toward openness.

You will be asked, whether by another or by your own heart, to share all. You'll have to decide if you will.

You'll be forced to move at another's pace. This often means slowing down. This demands the excruciating pain of waiting.

Your career, your dreams, and all your relationships will feel the effects of your choices. Your entire life will shift for this friend or this group of friends.

The cost is exorbitant, tremendous, outrageous.

Know this, though: Of those who've chosen this path and watched others avoid it, they agree on one thing: the cost of togetherness is minimal compared to the cost of walking alone.

Adam

- ☐ **What would you give up for a friend?**
- ☐ **What won't you? Why?**
- ☐ **Can you wait for a friend?**

THE OTHER COST, PART 1

"He who cannot forgive others breaks the bridge over
which he must pass himself."

— GEORGE HERBERT

Matthew 6:9-15 | Matthew 18:21-35 | Mark 11:22-25

Someone said that love primarily exists in a contractual way. Love means a commitment to which we bind ourselves. With love, we agree to give, receive, and seek forgiveness. We choose to continually reconcile, repair, and rebuild the relationship. We believe our partner will return again and again, no matter the cost.

The same nature underlies unforgiveness. We choose to sign a contract with binding terms, though no visible ceremony takes place. This contract, with its attendant vows, is subtle. Yet it brings with it unknown consequences.

When we decide not to forgive someone, isolation sets in. So do bitterness, misplaced anger, and alienation. We think our pride and dignity are worth the price, but we forsake so much of the richness of life. And we forsake a person, a friend.

Look at people who have chosen not to forgive; they're not hard to spot. Someone somewhere in the past wounded them. Since that time, they have planted a bitter root in their soul. The root needs nourishment to remain present, so it absorbs energy. Forgiveness would starve it quickly, but the root feeds on angry thoughts and memories. "It's just; it's my right. I remember what happened. I won't forget."

The difficult choice to forgive presents itself daily. But we need to smother the pride that tells us to cling to our grievances. There's more pain in forgiving, at least at first. We need to extract the wrong from our heart as we might shrapnel from our chest. If we don't, it slowly poisons us cell by cell.

We must forgive ourselves, our loved ones, and even our enemies. Otherwise, we place ourselves in bitter bondage. Few people are free from this prison. Daily we all observe the resulting tension and alienation around us.

We have the power to stop it: with each opportunity to forgive, to cancel debt, to heal wounds. Each time we choose forgiveness we renew the agreement.

You've signed the contract, and you agreed to its terms. Only you can break it.

Adam

———— ♦ ————

- ❏ **Whom have you not forgiven? Why?**
- ❏ **What would it take for you to forgive them?**
- ❏ **What price could you pay if you don't?**

THE OTHER COST, PART 2

"We went through the whole shebang alone.
We're islands now."

— DOUGLAS COUPLAND

| Deuteronomy 6:20-25 | Deuteronomy 30:15-20 | Luke 17:33 |

The November 2005 issue of *National Geographic* ran a story about the longest-living people groups in the world. The first group lives in Sardinia, Italy. The Sardinians eat pecorino cheese, drink red wine, and work hard. They also live closely together for their entire lives.

Married couples live longer than singles. Pet owners live longer than animal haters. Churchgoers live longer than non-churchgoers It seems the data suggests togetherness provides a more enhanced life than isolation --least in terms of length.

People who travel to poor, developing nations make several consistent observations. One, people in these countries know poverty intimately, while it is an abstract concept for most of us. Two, the people in economically impaired countries possess a profound joy incomprehensible to most of us in wealthy cultures. Three, that joy is directly tied to their sense of community.

In the modern, individualized West, we rarely think in terms of us and we. Instead, we think about me and being an individual rather than cuddling up to the inconvenience of the group. We have a life to live, you know?

But the poor tend to think more about others and less about themselves. What good is individual achievement when it's divorced from friends who might share in it? Why scale the ladder if you arrive at the top alone?

Jesus said, "Whoever loses his life will preserve it" (Luke 17:33).

Does this mean when we forget ourselves, we find something more worthwhile?

He also said those who seek to save their lives end up losing them. If Jesus is right, our approach isn't.

We can choose to go it alone. We can imitate John Wayne's characters, cowboys who needed no one. It sounds so romantic, like the Marlboro man, solitary to the backdrop of the setting sun. But at night, when the sun has set, the Marlboro Man has no one to tell him how cool he is, no one to share his cigarettes, and no one to keep him warm. If the indicators are correct, the Marlboro Man won't live too long.

Meanwhile, the Sardinians will live well, dining together on cheese and wine.

Adam

- ☐ What percentage of accomplishment in life has value outside of a social context?

- ☐ Why avoid a group?

- ☐ If you had to choose between unbelievable wealth and power or the company of a few very close friends, what would you choose and why?

THE FRUIT OF UNITY

"We are all in the same boat in a stormy sea,
and we owe each other a terrible loyalty."

— G.K. CHESTERTON

John 17:20-26	Colossians 3:12-14	Ecclesiastes 4:9-12

A few weeks ago, I sat in a spacious living room that was not spacious enough. The seating extended to the floor, end tables, and even other people. When all options were exhausted, the remainder of the large crowd squeezed into corners and stood in the entrance past the double doors. While the arrangement was not comfortable in the physical sense, the purpose of the gathering overshadowed the inconvenience.

College students, twenty-somethings, senior citizens, singles, married couples, retired people, career men and women, and representatives from all other disparate categories filled the room. No outside observer could have concocted a clear reason for why this mismatched crowd gathered. And yet the reason was not an event or some form of entertainment; the reason was a couple, a man and a woman who had loved every person in that room extravagantly.

We gathered to say goodbye as they left their home of the past two years, where they served as hosts of a house in Washington, DC. Although retired, they pursued this task with more effort and energy than any job before. They cooked, cleaned, and offered hospitality in heaping quantities.

Yet more than these defined roles, they loved. Always. They were the kind of people who always made space in their lives and their schedules when anyone called and wanted to just stop by and say hi. When I called once to schedule a time to see them, they invited me to join them on their Friday night date. (Incidentally, that evening with a seventy-year-old couple was the best date this twenty-something girl had been on in quite some time.)

They offered career advice, took me to breakfast, and asked pertinent questions about life. They cared, listened, and remembered. They loved honestly, and we recounted these times at the going away party that was more like a funeral as we mourn their departure from the city.

Jesus commanded us to live in unity with one another, to be good trees that bear good fruit. As I looked around the crowded room, the eclectic mixture of party guests transformed into a beautiful harvest of fruit, varied but all harvested at the point of ripeness by the love of this couple. They unified people with their availability and embrace of all.

Love produced the unity. It created a selective type of love that required possible recipients to be worthy enough, good-looking enough, able enough, or capable enough to offer something in return. The love that brought about this collection of people did not devise or discern who was "in" or "out." They loved everyone who came through their door.

As we sat and relished the final moments of time, it struck me that because of the love we received walking through that door, none of us wanted to walk out.

---•---

◻   **What prevents you from producing the fruit of unity?**

◻   **Why do you resist inclusion?**

◻   **How can you love others?**

DAY 20

A MAN, A NEIGHBOR AND GOD

"Without alienation, there can be no politics."

— ARTHUR MILLER

| John 13:21-38 | John 18:25-27 | John 21:4-19 |

Many have hailed Karl Marx as a genius for identifying alienation in the human condition. His philosophical and political treatises engage the topic of alienation as he looks at the worker's life in unchecked capitalism. But Marx saw nothing new. Two millennia prior, Jesus had already identified alienation, and more accurately. His solution involved not governments, but personal relations. His interactions with Peter bear this out.

Rather than focus on alienation based on social class, Jesus took a different tack. He sought to resolve alienation between two humans, between man and himself, between man and neighbor, and between man and God. Each of these relationships intimately ties into others. For our purposes, we'll take them one at a time. And because we think about ourselves most often, we'll deal with the first level of alienation immediately.

In John 8:1-11, Israel's morality police (teachers of the law and Pharisees) bring a woman to Jesus. They want to hold a trial for she's been caught having sex with a man who is not her husband. They don't bring her partner.

The only instance of Jesus writing occurs in this scene. We don't know what he writes in the sand. Perhaps he scratches the ten laws God gave Moses. This law stares at all parties nakedly and equally. Basically, He answered them saying something like, "He who is perfect can judge her."

One by one, the stones fall to the ground. "They began to go out one by one, beginning with the older ones"

Jesus remains. He looks at the woman. "Did no one condemn you? . . . I do not condemn you either."

Jesus was the only man who hadn't broken the law. The only wrong the Jews found with Him was His claim to be God's son. He's the only one who had every right to condemn her, but He didn't.

He released her to live anew. "Go. From now on sin no more."

When we realize that the one who deserves to condemn us forgives us, we can begin to accept and forgive ourselves. Such was the case for this woman. (The movie *The Passion* portrays Mary Magdalene as the woman in this scene.)

The act of forgiving ourselves doesn't begin in isolation. We need an outside voice to speak the words to us, to tell us we're forgiven, not cut off, not beyond redemption. And we need someone we can believe not just a fellow inmate in our personal prisons. We need someone perfect declaring, "You, me, we're all innocent!"

Jesus teaches us to reconcile with ourselves by showing us we're forgiven. He shows us God's love. He shows us we're loved. And if we'll follow, He'll lead us to loving the most unlovable, even ourselves.

—————◆—————

- ▢ **What do you dislike about yourself or not forgive yourself for?**
- ▢ **How would Jesus speak to you?**
- ▢ **Can you hear His words and believe them?**

BEARING A GRUDGE

"But these cuts I have,
they need love to help them heal."

— ELTON JOHN,
"DON'T LET THE SUN GO DOWN ON ME"

| Matthew 5:21-26 | Ephesians 4:25-27 | Luke 23:33-43 |

This is how I work: if someone slights me, I put up a wall. It might be small, to resemble the offense, but it performs the task of separating us. Eventually some people hurt me even more, and I build the wall higher to ensure that they stay out. I just can't let them do more damage.

It works like a credit card. I give people a certain line of credit. If they operate within their approved limit, their credit line grows. I give them more of me, of my time, resources, and heart.

If they exceed their limit at any given time, though, they incur a penalty of my anger that needs immediate payment. Compounding interest on the outstanding debt sets in. Adding up fast, and in short time, the debt becomes insurmountable. The relationship bankrupts because one party can't pay the debt, and the other won't forgive it.

"He has violated me too much for me to forgive." "I just can't give any more." "We're just too different." "We're not on good terms right now."

When the interest grows too high for one party to pay off, the relationship breaks, the credit is ruined.

How do we keep from losing credit in relationships? First, we could pay our debts immediately. We could admit wrongs. We could confront the painful and hard issues. We could seek forgiveness and give it quickly. Then we immediately reengage the relationship.

Another option is to work out the grievance over time. A tense moment here, a cold glimpse there, a biting comment or two could finally blow up, requiring a reconciliation. These situations are hard and painful, and tend to leave a scar. Or we could ignore the invisible elephant for a lifetime and live with the separation. This road ends in hard hearts and bitter roots. The grapes on this vine are sour and distasteful.

When paying relational debt, we need precision and care. Dealing with a wrong or a hurt doesn't justify reciprocated wounds. Let's not create more debt. Surgeons who extract glass from someone's foot use a scalpel not a saw. The same goes for dislodging the speck from a brother's eye or the log in our own.

Jesus teaches us to forgive others. He was the one who could love a criminal dying at the hands of justice. He could pray for those who nailed Him to a tree. While we clutch our list of hurts, He's busy canceling ours against God, against Him.

Forgiveness is not an issue of merit. But it is one of freedom. If you want liberty in your life, forgive. Forgive others and reconcile. Forgive yourself and walk free from the past. Understand that you've been forgiven.

And if this doesn't work, just know that Jesus ties our own forgiveness to our ability to forgive others. There's a great deal of liberty out there waiting to be given. Will we choose it?

◻   **What can't you forgive? Whom can't you? Why?**

◻   **Is it worth a supreme effort?**

◻   **Does forgiving mean forgetting? Why or why not?**

BELIEVING IN HIM

"I find it shelter to speak to you."

— EMILY DICKINSON

| Isaiah 59:1-3 | Isaiah 55:1-3 | Jeremiah 15:15-21 |

Now for the big question: How do we get right with God? How do we fix the relationship that has always felt a little off, a little broken?

The disclaimer is this: we're dealing in big matters, matters some would call divine. Despite our attempt to grasp everything we want to know, mystery will persist.

I'd love to offer you a computer program or theoretical formula like e=mc2 to solve the mystery, but I don't have that. None of us receive easy answers when trying to correct issues with God. Maybe we claim to have the formula, but it either falls woefully short or shrinks our God.

He's a person. People are complicated enough. Imagine the sophistication of an omniscient God.

John wrote his gospel with a keen eye toward knowing Jesus and knowing God. Look at some of the things John records Jesus saying:

> "This is the work of God, that you believe in Him whom He has sent" (6:29).

> "My teaching is not Mine, but His who sent Me" (7:16).

> "I have not come of Myself, but He who sent Me is true, whom you do not know. I know Him, because I am from Him, and He sent Me" (7:28-29).

> "You know neither Me nor My Father; if you knew Me, you would know My Father also" (8:19).

> "If God were your Father, you would love Me, for I proceeded forth and have come from God, for I have not even come on My own initiative, but He sent Me" (8:42).

> "Have I been so long with you, and yet you have not come to know Me, Philip? He who has seen Me has seen the Father . . . Do you not believe that I am in the Father, and the Father is in Me? (14:9,10)

Jesus keeps saying these things about Himself and about God.

He says, "God wants you to listen to Me. I am His messenger. If you know Me and listen to Me, you'll know God. Come to know Me that you might know God."

I heard someone say that people can only take you where they've been. If they haven't been someplace, they cannot take you there. Jesus says He's been there, that He *is* there. If we want to get there, Jesus must take us. But we must come to know Him, a person. Formulas and programs won't do it.

He is the way.

Adam

◻   **How do you think Jesus shows us God?**

◻   **How can you know Jesus better?**

◻   **Why should we get to know God?**

PROCEED

"What is friendship when all is said and done
but the giving and taking of wounds?"

— FREDERICK BUECHNER

| Hebrews 12:14-15 | Galatians 6:1-5 | Exodus 17:8-13 |

Someone I know recently completed his first triathlon. He didn't train, but he finished. Asked what he learned, he replied, "Run toward the pain."

An increasingly progress-oriented culture instructs its members to avoid, or eliminate, pain. Might we risk heresy and question the genius of avoiding all pain?

Pain plays a role in our growth. Great achievement almost necessarily begins in discomfort and soon moves into the pain of sacrifice. Look at the costs of building a business, earning a degree, winning in sports, purchasing a home, or managing a social career. Each of these includes some measure of pain. Birth, the grand metaphor, runs full of pain.

So do relationships. For unity that lasts, pain may play a part in its production. Typically, pain breaks the unspoken promise of togetherness and leads friends apart. What pain is that, though? That of hurts unaddressed? Of people seeing the reality of their actions and motives? Of dealing in the currency of humanity?

What of the pain of working toward agreement, resolution, and forgiveness? Might this pain draw us closer? Might it serve to bind us?

Any college football team playing in a major bowl game knows this. Ditto for a basketball team reaching the Final Four. Major League ball clubs playing in October and NBA or NHL teams playing in June have learned this lesson. With few exceptions, the fires of grueling discipline and sacrifice forged the bonds for these groups. It is the pain of practice and overcoming that unites them. What's more, the pain didn't prove too high a price; it reminded them that the price of quitting, walking away, and giving in is too high. The unity they'd earned with sacrifice mattered.

When you encounter difficulty with another human being, don't try to avoid further pain. You're better off working out the differences, resolving the conflict, and forgiving old hurts — even when it leads to painful places.

To move closer is no small feat. People will wound one another. But if we want a significant friendship with another person, we must take the steps into hard places. We must run toward the pain.

▢   Where do you find pain in relationships? How have you been hurt personally?

▢   How do you deal with it? Is this confrontation or retreat?

▢   How do you discern the difference between healthy pain and masochism?

DAY 24

A STATE OF UNION

Homer: Hey boy! Wanna play catch?
Bart: No thanks, Dad.
Homer: When a son doesn't want to play catch
with his father something is definitely wrong.
Grandpa Simpson: I'll play catch with you!
Homer: Go home.

— THE SIMPSONS

| Genesis 3-4 | Genesis 27 | Genesis 4:9 |

We really believe that self-sufficient independence and fulfilling relationships belong together. Might we have it wrong?

From the onset, we've sought equality with

God. Why should we live under His authority? Adam and Eve asked this question.

The answer arrived quickly. Their first-born son killed his younger brother. The human race clearly has its issues.

In this world, independence marks one as strong. Above all, we need to look good or avoid looking bad. Talk about others, but not to them. Manipulate others to benefit and protect you. This begins to touch on our thought process.

Compounding our problems, we depart from the historical mainstream as we exalt the individual over the group. What I want—my education, my career, my money, my car, my home—dictates the direction of my life. Few people stay tied to the family or community in which we grow up. Immigrants quickly adopt this attitude, ensconcing themselves in a culture that pushes individuals further "ahead" and thus apart.

Something greater than me exists. And not just God. Catholic and Greek Orthodox faithful comprehend this. Many Jews and Muslims do as well. Some true communists, probably most tribes in "developing" nations, and the mafia all grasp this principle: the community's value far outpaces the sum of its parts. The community can impart meaning and identity to the individual, to the faith, to one's world.

Still, our thoughts turn back to us. Mine move back to me, as yours do to you. I don't need anyone. They'd only impede my progress.

Yes, we're getting there. We chase wealth, influence, networks, and status. We all find ourselves reaching and climbing higher. And look at what we find as we arrive: a third of us make it to our twenty-fifth wedding anniversary, drug and alcohol abuse continue unabated, crime and violence remain with us, and suicide persists as a leading cause of death among young people.

Some say we've come a long way since the beginning of time. Have we really? Are we any better? As a collective? As individuals?

Adam

———◆———

- To what extent do you see your relationships as an end?

- Or are they simply another rung in the ladder we climb?

- Could relationships be the ultimate end?

CLAIMED

"After landing his invasion forces on the shores of
some country, the 16th Century Spanish conquistador
Cortes would immediately burn his own boats.
He was sending his army a message:
'We can't turn back.
Either we succeed here, or we die here.'
Excuses were not an option."

— LOU HOLTZ

| Galatians 3:26-29 | Ephesians 2:11-18 | 1 Corinthians 1:10-17 |

In the picturesque, though critically panned, movie *Far and Away* Tom Cruise's character stakes a flag in the dirt of Oklahoma amidst a land rush. For a moment, the camera focuses on this banner.

Like a wedding band, the symbol represents an inner pledge. This mere flag declared that someone claimed this land. Someone decided to work it, to sweat and bleed over it, and to live or die by its success.

I think of this image often. When presented with the choice to proceed or withdraw, to advance or retreat, to give up or give all, I ponder this image. It is the perfect image when in the pursuit of a degree or job, working toward a goal in athletics, moving to a new and occasionally terrifying city or country, and especially in relationships.

Staking a flag in the ground says, "This is mine. I'm responsible for it, and I choose to remain here. I choose to share all, to know and to be known." The claim pronounces, "I'll know you, all of you: the frightening and unacceptable parts as well as the glorious and spectacular. I'll allow you to know all of me as well. This is my pledge."

We avoid such bold strokes of living. "That's personal," we say to our friends. When did these couple of words become acceptable among friends? Is friendship not the most personal aspect of life where we are most fully persons? Can we not begin to speak of the unmentionables of life? If not in friendship, where? We shouldn't have to pay someone to tell us the truth about who we are.

The most personal act we can choose is a life of friendship. Life together requires a claim. It requires a stake in the ground, a flag for you and others to see. It demands your intention, your purposefulness, your shout from hilltops, "I'm here! To fight and live and even die for this!"

We each have our own land to claim. It rests in the bonds of family and friendships all about us. It is ours to stake out, not to wait to inherit. Let us choose it as our own. Let us go there willing to die.

Adam

◻ With whom have you chosen to speak about everything?

◻ What keeps you from doing so with anyone? With more than one? To what extent will you choose to allow someone to know all of you—and to what extent will you accept them?

QUESTION UNITY, QUESTION YOU

"One who asks a question is a fool for five minutes; one who does not ask a question remains one forever."

— CHINESE PROVERB

| Job 38:1-3 | Jeremiah 17:5-10 | Proverbs 14:5-6 |

In what do I want to invest my life? Work? Money? Achievement? People?

Do I want friends?

Are friends better than isolation?

Are two better than one? Why?

What have I done to be part of a group? What have I done to deserve to be out, excluded, abandoned, expelled, or avoided?

What can Jesus teach me about the above?

What is essential for friendship to exist in my life? To last? To matter?

Am I willing to work at a friendship? Despite the inevitable pain? Despite the taxing efforts?

Why am I working so hard to protect my information?

How do I get to know it more intimately? Do I want to?

At what level am I committed? Do others know this? Do I say it?

Do I forgive? Quickly? Why not?

Have I asked someone to forgive me?

Do I have sufficient time and energy to nurse a grudge, to hold onto bitterness?

Do I believe love involves sacrifice? Will I?

Do friendships need openness? Will I lean toward that versus protecting myself?

Can I love others as I love myself? Why does Jesus tell us to do this?

How do I dodge confrontation?

Can I submit or defer to a friend without resenting him or her?

Could Jesus be at the center of a relationship? Should He be? Why?

Is He at the center? If not, what is?

Would I shift my life for a friend?

When I confront someone, do I use a sword or a scalpel?

Will I choose to share all? Of myself? Of my possessions?

Adam

DAY 27

PERSONAL EMANCIPATION

"Piglet sidled up to Pooh from behind.
'Pooh!' he whispered. 'Yes, Piglet?'
'Nothing,' said Piglet, taking Pooh's paw.
'I just wanted to be sure of you.'"

— A. A. MILNE

Colossians 3:12-17	1 Corinthians 13:8-13	John 21:15-19

As usual, he was late, and I was antsy. But he finally showed up and sat next to me at the bar. We spoke openly of marriage, friends, sex, God, money, work, and each other. We imbibed our usual spirits, downed marvelous burgers. And then it came.

The doubt.

I couldn't help but wonder if this relationship could continue outside the bar. Most people would say we had a deep friendship, but we lacked something. To function outside the pub where most of our interactions took place involved risk. The proposition was perilous because we might not function well or smoothly in another context. What if it feels awkward? What if we lose the bar magic?

Life's too short to fear the answers.

A similar situation occurred with another friend I met playing football. A few years older and seemingly a world apart, our conversations consistently circled football's Cover 2 zone defense, the SEC, and the Italians' superiority over the French.

As we have each grown, we've woven boldness into our discussions. We ask, "How can I know you more?" There comes the occasional brick wall of silence or uncertainty, but we continue forward, asking new questions, sharing different experiences in unique contexts. We eat together. We bring our families into our friendship. We play together, travel together, and introduce each other to friends.

We had to walk off the field to know each other fully, as men, as people, as friends. Stepping off the figurative context of the field, we stepped into the literal experience of each other's worlds. We entered life together. But it meant we couldn't stay where we had been. It was awkward at times. It proved painful and slow. But it grew.

John Ortberg penned the book *If You Want to Walk on Water, You've Got to Get Out of the Boat*. I haven't read it, but I like the title. If we want to move ahead in knowing someone, we need to risk failure. Sure, Peter began to sink, but Jesus caught him and asked, "Where is your faith?" He didn't ask, "Why'd you get out of the boat? Are you nuts?"

We should move our friendships into new contexts and do so for friendship. We need to deal with the uncomfortable to create new levels of comfort. We must tell the terrible truth. Ask the question, "How do we know each other?" We must risk failing, so we don't risk missing the full person altogether.

You can't stay here.

Adam

⎯⎯⎯◆⎯⎯⎯

- ❑ **Think of one friend. What are you afraid to ask him or her?**
- ❑ **What are you afraid he or she will ask?**
- ❑ **What do you risk by speaking the truth or hearing it?**

DAY 28

WHY TOGETHER

"It is of infinite moment, that you should properly
estimate the immense value of your
national Union to your collective
and individual happiness."

— GEORGE WASHINGTON'S FAREWELL ADDRESS

| Matthew 5:21-26 | John 17 | 1 John 4:16-21 |

John 17 records Jesus' prayer for those who believe in Him. He asks one thing of the Father for them: "That they may be one, just as We are one" (v. 22).

Scan the religious landscape. You'll see religions, and within those there are denominations and sects. Within denominations and sects, you'll notice further individuation as people differentiate themselves according to dress or interests. Dialogue between religions or denominations might appear theologically soft or insufficiently provincial. Its scarcity increases.

Why did Jesus pray for unity?

Our first sin, rebellious independence, has led us here, to the struggle with one another. This willful independence cuts us off from God. It alienates us from one another. Because of this, He sent us out of the garden.

The Father imparts the ultimate timeout: "Get out and stay out. Figure out how to get along. Then you can begin to understand Me, what I want, why you're here. Till then, work it out among yourselves."

At the end of Matthew's gospel, Jesus says, "Where two or three gather in My name, I am there" (Matthew 18:20). Later, He recites the second commandment, "Love your neighbor as yourself," which is like the first: "Love the Lord your God" (Matthew 22:36, 39).

We couldn't understand relational unity then. We still can't. Thus, Jesus gave us His words and example of how we might reconnect with one another and with God. While we might treat relationships with God and others as exclusive from one another, for Jesus, they're inseparable.

This makes sense, especially when one considers the crazy things Jesus tells us to do. Can we do anything He says without the help of someone else? Love an enemy? Offer a cheek to a fist? Forgive seventy times seven?

This unity idea pleases Jesus. He wants us together. He wants us closer to Him. But we must make it right with one another to have it right with Him. Till we do, we remain cut off, shut out.

Our love for each other is the piety God desires.

Adam

———◆———

- ◻ Do you believe oneness pleases God? Why or why not

- ◻ What is your idea of oneness or unity?

- ◻ How does this line up with the Lord's idea?

BEARING FRUIT & ABIDING

WALKING WITH THE LORD

"As you walk with Jesus, resting your head on His heart,
you will learn to know His Word, His will, and His ways.
You will want to obey Him, not out of forced compliance,
but out of heartfelt connection. Your joy will abound as
you remain in His love."

— SUE DETWEILER

| Genesis 5:24 | Genesis 6:9 | Micah 6:8 |

Reading through the Old Testament one cannot miss the references to people who "walked with God." Enoch walked so closely with God that in the end God took him straight into His presence.

But what does this mean, exactly? What does it look like for us to walk day by day with our Maker? After all, we can't see Him or touch Him. We cannot feel His form tangibly, and most of the time we cannot hear His voice audibly (although some have).

As I ponder the question of what it means to truly walk with God, I am reminded of a sticky note I put on my mirror years ago. It says simply this:

> Put on the Lord Jesus Christ and allow Him to live through me.
> Stay holy and set apart in your thoughts and actions.
> Be inspired every day to walk with Him and pass on His blessings.
>
> — January 1, 2013.

This little pink sticky note bears the scars of its age. It's been tattered and splattered, as well as torn around its edges. These words that came to me on New Year's Day 2013 breathe life into my soul every morning. I remember that I was praying and trying to simply listen for some sort of message from the Almighty. The words that tumbled out onto the sticky note are the exact expression that flowed naturally into my consciousness in that moment. I still recall the feelings of peace and love that washed over me.

This short note became the game plan for my life. I desire every morning to "put on the Lord Jesus Christ and allow Him to live through me." Throughout the day, I attempt to keep my thoughts and actions pure and set apart from simply worldly ones. I constantly ask the Lord to quicken my spirit and inspire me to "walk with Him and pass on His blessings."

Although these are the words the Lord gave me, I realize that He has a special and unique design for each person who would choose to walk with Him. In the end, we will live a fruitful life—one filled and fulfilled.

————— ♦ —————

▫ **How are you walking through life now, and is your life bearing good fruit?**

▫ **What should your walk with God look like?**

▫ **What words would the Lord give you to draw upon as you walk with Him?**

MANKETTI TREE

"When peace like a river attendeth my way.
When sorrows like sea billows roll.
Whatever my lot, thou hast taught me to say,
it is well, it is well, with my soul."

— HORATIO SPATFORD,
"IT IS WELL WITH MY SOUL"

| Matthew 6:25-34 | Hebrews 5:11-14 | Psalm 1 |

Little vegetation grows in the deserts of Africa. Arid conditions and sweltering temperatures make survival nearly impossible for anything other than some scraggly shrubbery. Yet in this veritable wasteland, the Manketti tree manages to eke out an existence. These trees grow strong and wide across the windswept savannas of Chad, Mali, Niger, and Uganda. They spread their far-reaching limbs that produce white flowering blooms and mongongo nut, one of the most essential nuts of socioeconomic and nutritive importance in that region of Africa.

Beyond the visible portion of the tree—the stout trunk and widely splayed limbs—the sustainability of the Manketti exists in its root system. Unlike many trees in more kind and lush climates, the Manketti's root system does not extend to occupy a vast surface area. Instead, it grows one long taproot that plunges deep into the earth until it reaches water. When drought persists, the tree survives. It is rooted in something deeper and survives on something more than the fickle nature of daily precipitation.

Our lives bring difficulties. Friends fail us; our lives lie beyond our control. Stresses and tensions press in from all angles. Our family members fail to understand us, and we misunderstand them regularly. We realize that jobs never fully satisfy, and even the most appealing ones provide their fair share of drudgery. The paradoxes continue when fun proves completely un-fun, and things meant to bring rest bring anxiety.

We look to a variety of things to ensure sustenance and survival. We demand continued supply and thus grow our roots near the surface to glean from the fickle waters that fall from the sky. But what if these rains never come? What if they skip a day? Or a week? Or a month?

The truth is this: We depend on the undependable.

Unless we plunge our taproots into deep streams that nourish despite the challenges of life, our existence will depend on the fickle nature of the uncontrollable. We will wither when life does not satisfy. Our green leaves will turn a brittle brown when friends fail and family misunderstands.

Our failures will translate to death unless we are rooted in something deeper.

Amy

————◆————

▫ **In what are you rooted?**

▫ **Where do you find your sustenance?**

▫ **How can you deepen your roots?**

TOO MUCH, TOO QUICKLY, TOO SOON

"Moderation is the inseparable companion of wisdom,
but with it genius has not even a nodding acquaintance."

— CHARLES CALEB COLTON

| Matthew 13:5-6 | Matthew 13:8-9 | Galatians 6:7-10 |

We want it all. We want it now.

We have never been good at waiting. We like things quickly, and we realize that we are textbook examples of American instant gratification. The glorious finale appeals more than the tedious process. And yet the process cannot be eliminated—growth takes time. We've learned the hard way.

In second grade we embarked on the exciting science adventure, at least that is what our teacher deemed this experiment, thinking that the enticing name would convince us energetic eight-year-olds that botany was fun. We would plant our own seeds and watch them grow. We buried the seeds in rich, black soil; watered them appropriately; and waited for the blooms to grow.

I waited for days. Nothing sprouted. Classmates of mine, similarly disillusioned with the process, concocted rapid-growth plans that seemed quite plausible in their young, scientifically uninformed minds. If a little water was good, more water was better. If sunlight prompted growth, excessive brightness could only cause more growth. Between the lethal combination of drowning and overexposure, our seeds never sprouted.

Years have passed since this initial botanical failure, and while I have yet to retest my gardening skills, I am fascinated by the process of planting a seed, virtually nothing, and having something grow from it.

A few months ago, I talked with a friend who grew up on a farm. He explained the science behind weed killers. I had always thought the chemicals annihilated the weeds because of their lethal toxicity. Weed killers work not because they introduce something bad to the plant, but instead because they provide too much good.

Trying to preserve the limited soil and water in a field for crops, farmers use chemicals to kill weeds. They spray the substance on the unwanted plants, and within a few minutes it withers and dies. At first glance, it appears that the chemical prevented the plant from growing when in fact it performed just the opposite: it accelerated the growth in the weed so significantly that its demands for water and other nutrients exceeded its ability to obtain them.

The weed grew itself to death.

We love growth. We love to see movement and change, as evidenced by our consistent resolve to keep making New Year's resolutions, although we inevitably abandon them. Perhaps the problem lies not in the resolutions but in our ability to sustain them. Growth succeeds when it is steady, when the nutrients and the resources are ample for the desired end.

———————◆———————

- ☐ **What good things prevent growth in your life?**
- ☐ **In what areas do you want to grow?**
- ☐ **How can you facilitate that growth?**

DAY 32

BOBBLEHEADS, BIG HANDS, BALANCED LIFE

"I've lost something. I want to try to find it again."

— JOHN STEINBECK

| Ephesians 4 | Colossians 3:12-17 | 2 Peter 1:5-9 |

Bobblehead Night makes for one of the best nights on any sports team's calendar. Is there anything cooler than receiving a doll whose oversized and ever-smiling head bounces endlessly? We look at any bobblehead, laugh, and then in relief think, "Gosh, I'm glad my head isn't that big. I couldn't get out of bed in the morning, poke my head in the fridge, or find clothes with a suitable neckline ."

Having a bobblehead-sized head would compare to the giant foam hands with the index finger pointing up. While fun to wear at baseball games, a hand that size wouldn't work in everyday life. It wouldn't fit in our pockets. It would make holding a cell phone difficult. And it couldn't grasp tweezers.

Our gifts, talents and life pursuits can become bobbleheads and big hands. They can grow too large and lead to an out-of-balance life.

What is life out of balance? It's when a person only develops his or her strengths or pursues one aspect of life. It's a hall of fame coach sending tapes of his family's dinners to the office. It's someone working out more than once a day when they're not a professional athlete. It's being "too busy" for a relationship.

People who are out of balance neglect working on their weaknesses because strengthening them proves difficult. They know only one thing; they are happy to be only one thing, to play only one role, and to wear only one hat. They try to convince themselves that this one aspect will suffice.

Be more. Be more than a student. Be a pray-er, an evangelist, a teacher, a pastor, a president, a soldier, a frat guy, a businessman, a deacon, a cleric, a scholar, an investor, a fan, an owner, an artist, a carpenter, a musician. Be a complete person. Be a whole person, not just a player of one role.

There is a greater wholeness in being part of a larger body of people. We have more than one role to play. A hand points, grasps, reaches, and touches, but it also must remain connected to the wrist, the arm, and the rest of the body. We each have a role to play. The connection grants our gifts their value or lack thereof—no matter how seemingly crucial they are.

Let us not remain people with outsized gifts. This only leads us to life out of balance, making us incapable of life together. A teacher, when connected to the community, also becomes a friend, a sister, a brother, a helper, a servant, a leader. The athlete becomes a husband, a deacon, a mentor, a coach. We each become more and more human.

Does this mean we should deny our gifts? No, certainly not. It means training them and remembering that the gift itself is not the end. The aim is learning to use the talents, abilities, and opportunities and contribute to the whole, to bring something to the community, because the community is the point. A life in balance is the point. Becoming whole by coming together is the point. Bobbleheads and big hands are not.

Adam

☐ **Have you focused on one area of your life to the detriment of other areas?**

☐ **What is this doing to your ability to relate to others, to exercise and to grow others' gifts, to learn more about who you are?**

SNOZZBERRIES

"A big elm in a single season might make as many as six million leaves, wholly intricate, without budging an inch; I couldn't make one."

— ANNIE DILLARD

| John 15:1-8 | Luke 6:43-45 | John 6:28-29 |

In the original movie *Willy Wonka and the Chocolate Factory* (the old one with the terrible special effects), the lucky children who tour Willy Wonka's candy factory visit various departments of the production facility. Confections abound, including, but certainly not limited to, gummy bears larger than bowling balls.

At one juncture, they enter a room of brightly colored wallpaper depicting vivid fruit. Wonka tells the children to lick the wallpaper because the "Strawberries really taste like strawberries, and the snozzberries really taste like snozzberries." The children all stare agape as he describes this delicacy, until he mentions the snozzberries. The trance breaks. One particularly disbelieving youth declares, "There's no such thing as a snozzberry."

Visions of fruit also appear in the Scriptures. Good trees bear good fruit. Bad trees bear bad fruit. The fruits of the Spirit stem from lives lived in Christ. Fruit conveys, in tangible form, the intangible sweetness of a life well lived, with juice more succulent than candy and refreshment better than anything artificially produced. But how does this fruit appear? And what dictates the form in which it grows?

A few years ago a friend discussed the imagery of God as the vine and us as the branches. He questioned me, "What is our job as the branch?" Always quick with a response, I replied, "To produce fruit."

He looked at me and simply said, "No." I doubled back in my mind, baffled as to what I missed. He explained, "Our sole job is to stay connected to the vine. Then the fruit just comes."

I thought about these words for a while. My first response bordered on anger. All I must do is hang on?! I want to produce something, and I want to know what it is that I produce!

Then my quasi-anger transformed into relief.

All I need to do is hang on. The fruit comes. I'm no longer forced to attempt the impossible task of understanding, implementing, and accomplishing fruit production. I no longer must worry about whether grapes, oranges, apples, or strawberries sprout from my branches.

I just need to hang on. My focus can be singular and sound. My energy can be dedicated to one thing instead of divided anxiously, and ineffectively, among many. God knows the fruit He wants me to produce, and perhaps it will be something radical, something beyond my comprehension. Perhaps it may be a snozzberry.

- □ **Why is it hard to believe that our purpose is singular and simple?**
- □ **What fruit is being produced in your life?**
- □ **What is your favorite fruit?**

IRA

"The birth and growth of the spirit, in those who
are attentive to their own inner life, are slow and
exceedingly painful. Our mothers are racked with the
pains of our physical birth; we ourselves suffer the
longer pains of our spiritual growth."

— MARY ANTIN

| Luke 6:39-49 | Matthew 7:7-29 | James 3:9-18 |

In this life, we save for a later date. We put the products of our time and labor in some box for safekeeping. We call those boxes 401(k)s, pensions, or Social Security. We put away the fruits of our efforts for a day when they're needed. They comprise our fortune, waiting for our arrival at that future date.

Jesus told His followers to store treasure in heaven. Invest there. Tap into an IRA upon your arrival. Heaven's banks, he said, are more secure than Swiss accounts.

What makes for a spiritual retirement fund? Jesus describes a plant bearing fruit, and His words are as gentle as His "hate your family" remarks. When it comes to fruit, however, He said it sprouts from connecting to Him (see John 15:5). The products of our life, when we connect to Him, are invisible (see Ephesians 5:16-26). Our production runs through Him and comes from Him.

We connect to Him as we talk to Him, think about Him, and listen to Him. We follow His lead and learn from His teaching. This develops rapport. This leads to fruit bearing. The time and effort put into these pursuits produce spiritual fruit, and treasure in heaven.

What is spiritual fruit? What is treasure in heaven?

Nothing we can see goes beyond the grave. Therefore, the things we value—wealth, fame, physical beauty, stature—cannot pass muster with what Jesus values. Most of us spend our time, money, and energy on things we cannot secure.

If we're spirit, though, the spirit part of us will stay with us: love, goodness, wisdom, joy, peace, mercy, grace, and fidelity. These intangibles, Paul says, represent the Spirit's outcome, its fruit, in our lives.

We're headed to a day when we'll look at our lives and ask, "What have I accumulated? What have I done? What has been the payoff? What have I become? Have all these years of working for money produced anything worthwhile?"

Will we look at what we've saved and say, "I put it in the wrong place?" Will they meet the needs of that future date?

Jesus never told us not to work for money. But He made clear those things for which we should be working.

Adam

- ☐ What are you doing to store treasures for heaven?

- ☐ Do you value them?

- ☐ To what degree do you value Jesus' teachings? To what degree do you value Jesus?

SEASONS

"I stepped off the plane a few hours ago, arriving in
the strangely sub-arctic temperatures of Baltimore
after departing from a balmy Los Angeles afternoon.
Subconsciously I willed the plane to pivot 180 degrees
and return to the Pacific Coast: to the beaches, ocean
breezes, air that smelled of flowers, and trees teeming
with ripe avocados and robust oranges."

— HENRI NOUWEN

| Ecclesiastes 3:1-8 | Luke 13:6-9 | 2 Timothy 4:1-5 |

Even though I grew up in the wintry blizzards of Michigan, I was out of practice for the harsh climactic dichotomy I experienced earlier this evening. I renounced winter. I renounced cold. I renounced four seasons, one of which registered as highly miserable.

Yet, as I renounced the current season in the four-season system, I took comfort in knowing that the next would soon arrive. A new season awaits. While the trees wear a mask of winter deadness, leafless and naked, life still holds the potential of green inside the branches. Crocuses count the degrees until they stoically emerge as the first flowers of the season.

Hardy coniferous trees hold their evergreen needles continually, but they want to bask in warmness and exchange their snowy covering to instead hold the nests of birds awaiting the hatching of their young.

The hope of this dreary season resides in the assured potential of what is to come. What looks like dreariness and death may be an encasement that houses the coming of new life.

We are not unlike our surroundings. We too experience seasons. At times our lives bear the obvious fruit and flowering of summer excess. At other times, the only form of life in us is the unseen green center inside our branches. While we refuse to welcome the frigid cold, and what looks like stunted or stagnant progress perhaps is a necessary stage.

Perhaps we must know winter in order to be ready for, and appreciate, spring. Although the dormant times are painful, perhaps they prove necessary for the times of visible growth. Perhaps they slow us down and prompt us to search, question and care.

In Ecclesiastes, wise King Solomon writes there is "a season for every activity under the heavens" (Ecclesiastes 3:1 NIV). He allows that there is "a time to be born and a time to die" (v. 2). The opposites exist. Death and life are mutually necessary parts of the journey. He continues that there is "a time to weep and a time to laugh" (v. 4). Tears and joy exist in inextricable combination.

Winter comes, but spring promises to follow.

Amy

———◆———

□ **What season are you experiencing in life right now?**

□ **What is God teaching you in that place?**

□ **How do you normally respond to "winter" times?**

DAY 36

TOO SIMPLE

"Dear God, I want to be just like my Daddy
when I grow up but not with so much hair all over."

— SAM, LETTERS TO GOD FROM CHILDREN

John 15:1-17	Psalm 92:12-15	Luke 18:15-17

Some people remain in an esoteric world that has little value. Few people I know have a gift of making the apparently complex understandable and livable. Jeremy being one of them, I called him.

"What is Jesus telling us with this passage in John 15? Abide? Remain? Would it not have been easier to say something like, 'Stay connected to me'?" I asked.

"I don't think Jesus meant for it to be so complex," he said. "We try to spiritualize things. We try to add to the details because we've grown accustomed to such a complex world. It's not too complicated for us; it's too simple."

He then started talking about what it looks like. Sometimes I just need a picture.

"We're each unique," he said. "And because of that, it looks unique for each person. Everyone has a distinct abiding in Jesus. We just walk it out with Jesus. He says, 'Come along, and we'll work out the details on the way.' If we have some image of 'what it looks like,' we'd miss the point—being with Him and learning from Him."

As he spoke, I looked over my shoulder. He started talking about an oak tree and time, and I couldn't hear his point because I saw it. I saw the thing itself.

A mother held her infant girl to herself.

This girl lives in her mother. She needs her mother's help for the most mundane things, from eating to sleeping to dressing. When she makes a decision, she asks, "How will Mommy feel about this? How will this affect her?"

She cries when her mother leaves. She clings and yearns to be near her, intrinsically grasping for one who represents life in her small world. She desires to grow up to be like her mother, and she can't imagine a future without her.

Because she lives in her mother, her mother lives in her.

The mother remains in the little girl even as she becomes a young lady and eventually a woman. The daughter will look and act like her mother. She'll think like her in time, and she'll speak like her. She'll frequent the same locales and take on similar relationships. She'll become the kind of woman her mother is.

What happens between the moment when I saw the child and when she is a mother herself is the walk they'll take together. They'll take methodic steps and have meaningful conversations along the way. The uniqueness lies there. The details remain for the mother and daughter to work out over time, as they remain in each other.

Adam

————◆————

▢   **Do you make walking with Jesus more complex than you need? How so?**

▢   **What should it look like for you?**

▢   **Whom do you want living in you?**

GROWTH

"There came a time when the risk to remain tight in the bud was more painful than the risk it took to blossom."

— ANAIS NINN

| John 15 | James 3:9-18 | Colossians 1:9-14 |

Y ou can't make yourself grow. You cannot tell muscle, sinew, and bone to expand. You don't possess this power.

You can, however, make for an environment that fosters growth. You can ingest healthy food. You can exert yourself in such a way that the body responds with growth. You can rest so that the body has time to recover. You can supplement a healthy diet with creatine, protein powders, and a dash of HGH. These together create an environment for growth.

As much as women want to tone thighs and hips and men want to build muscle in their arms and chests, we all want to grow as people. The visible change serves as a physical manifestation of the inner growth we desire.

We grow weary of tempers, self-obsession, childishness, foolish fears, and insecurities. Who wants to remain in that place? Besides, we cannot will it so.

Jesus employed a metaphor of a vine and its branches. The vine provides the water and nutrition for the branches. They do not sustain themselves. All kinds of life flows through the vine. To cut a branch from a vine is to kill it. Remember, He's the vine, and we're the branches.

A camp counselor once showed my friend, Amy, two sticks. One was old, gray, and brittle. The other was fresh, blossoming, and green in the center.

"Which of these two is alive?" she asked. Amy quickly pointed to the one from which the leaves sprang. "No," she replied. "Both are dead. Neither is connected to the branch."

Growth results naturally from intimacy in relationships. The greatest growth stems from a closeness to Jesus.

Two things we need to remember. The first is that seasons for growth will come, and seasons without growth will come. Watching nature's yearly routine reveals this.

The second is that growth itself is not our aim. Growth enables us to stand more closely to our beloved. Growth is the stripping away of selfishness. It is the acclimatization to staying near someone else for extended periods. We grow for intimacy's sake. We don't seek intimacy for growth's sake.

Adam

- How have you grown in the last year?
- What fostered the growth?
- Why do you want to grow?

DAY 38

HOLY HOUSE, HOLLOW HOUSE

"The church is nearby, the road is icy; the bar is far away, but I will walk carefully."

— RUSSIAN PROVERB

| Luke 13:6-9 | Matthew 13:1-23 |

On either end of my block stand two church buildings, two small but elegant cathedrals. They have stood here for a long time but now remain unvisited and empty.

Seeing a prime location and lovely architecture, a developer purchased them. He reworked the interiors and transformed cavernous, vacant sanctuaries into a lucrative investment. These once-historic churches now provide sanctuary for the few people who call these luxury condos home.

When did God stop visiting these brick houses of His? When did He quit stopping by to visit His friends? Why did He leave? Or why did the people leave? Did these churches lose their mojo?

Jesus said, "Remain in me, and I will remain in you" (John 15:4 NIV) Did He lie?

We kept showing up. Someone, at least, continued going to His house. One might compare the disconnect to a broken marriage. Some couples can keep up appearances for the marriage, but they have long since abandoned it.

They lived together, wore the rings, paid the bills, and raised the kids. But they did not speak. They no longer confessed sin or sentiment. They left the house for the job or hobby. This proved far easier than admitting it was over and moving out, letting go. They play an adult version of house, but they fail to engage in real life.

Back to God again: Did He lie? If we had kept showing up and doing what people of faith do—praying liturgy, singing the songs, giving money, taking communion—would He renege?

Or did we leave the relationship without moving out of the house? Maybe we packed up our heart and commitment. We thought that if we just stopped by now and then, we could ignore the fact that we had quit reaching out to hold His hand. We had quit asking for His help. We had quit thinking so highly of Him. And we could maintain the appearance.

But we lost the promise. We broke the contract. And the love our God gave would go with Him. He'd be a stranger.

He promised. We didn't. As humans, composites of sinners and saints, we fear the promise. We struggle to fulfill those we make, despite our desires. Then we leave. We just don't move out. We live alone in beautiful luxury condos with no congregation, no friends to visit, no God to come by.

◻ **Have we left Him and not moved out?**

◻ **Does He inhabit our lives? How? Why?**

◻ **Do we need to reconcile with Him? How?**

GOD BEFORE SELF

POWERS THAT BE

"Obedience alone gives the right to command."

— RALPH WALDO EMERSON

| Romans 13:1-7 | 1 Timothy 2:1-4 | Matthew 8:8-10 |

I remember vividly one scenario where I witnessed the transformation of the citizenry and its view of presidential authority. In January of 1981, I helped plan the National Prayer Breakfast, and our small staff was given a tour of the Washington Hilton Hotel in Washington, DC.

One part of this tour stood out to me. In the receiving area where the president could engage in private conversations with VIPs before entering the three-thousand-seat International Ballroom, was an unmarked private door on the outside of the hotel, which led to the reception area. It seemed plain, especially since the president made his entry across an open sidewalk and in the door. I mostly forgot about my impression until two months later, on March 30, 1981.

A group of us was working in the inner city, doing much-needed rehab work on inner-city housing. On the way home one day, we heard over the radio that President Ronald Reagan had just been shot at the Washington Hilton Hotel.

My mind darted back to the memory of my tour there. I could envision exactly where it happened. What I found most interesting, though, was the way the episode crystallized Americans' love for this president. Friends of mine who considered Reagan unworthy of the presidency suddenly developed a respect for him.

The president was rushed to the nearest hospital, where he was operated on and began his slow recovery. One of his White House staff, Press Secretary James Brady, was hit by one of the bullets in his head. His life was in jeopardy.

Both recovered, but Brady's brain injury affected him for the rest of his life. The president seemed to make a full recovery in the months that followed.

We love some of our leaders, and others we don't. What fascinates me is how we decide whether someone is a good leader or a bad leader. It may have to do with their views, with their race, or their family connections, or their political party.

The Scriptures instruct us to honor those in authority, whether they are popular or not. We are commanded to pray for them, whether we like them or not, whether we agree with their platforms or not. We are told by Paul to pay taxes and respect. Then we shall live in peace.

Brad

- ☐ How do you generally respond to people in leadership?
- ☐ Do you pray for them?
- ☐ When is it admissible to rebel against authority?

THE ID

"It is a serious thing to live in a society of possible gods and goddesses, to remember that the dullest and most uninteresting person you talk to may one day be a creature which, if you saw it now, you would be strongly tempted to worship, or else a horror and a corruption such as you now meet, if at all, only in a nightmare. All day long we are, in some degree, helping each other to one or other of these destinations."

— C.S. LEWIS, "THE WEIGHT OF GLORY"

| Colossians 3:1-4 | Matthew 10:38-39 | Romans 12:1-2 |

Philosopher Sigmund Freud described the id aspect of our personalities. This is the part of the unconscious that cares only for himself or herself and is consumed with taking, seldom giving anything back. This lower, or base, part of our personality has received much literary attention. Thomas Merton, for example, wrote extensively about the true authentic self. It's opposing side was the false, or fictional, self.

We need to understand both sides of ourselves.

First, we must grasp that we are capable of all kinds of evil, as we are fallen beings. Yet, at the same time, the Scriptures tell us that we have been reborn into a new life that God sees as perfect. When we look at our false self, we realize that its basic instinct is narcissism, which seems to be currently at an all-time high in America. God exhorts us to humble ourselves first, so He may exalt us (Matthew 23:12). Our narcissism is then quenched.

Our heart constantly battles with our mind about who we really are. When we are redeemed, Paul tells us that our life is hidden with Christ in God (Colossians 3:3). It is redeemed, and when God looks at us in that condition, He sees only Jesus. We understand this knowledge deep in our heart, but the physical mind has not caught up.

As Paul points out, we are to offer ourselves as a "living sacrifice," in order to be transformed in the way we think (Romans 12:1-2). Our heart understands the reality that we have already been perfected by Jesus. As we go through our lives on planet earth, we are hopefully renewing our minds to fall in line with that thought.

The problem with a living sacrifice is that it is constantly crawling off the altar. Paul realizes that our souls have been saved, but our minds need to be constantly transformed to the image of God. This involves dethroning the self. The id must go. When speaking to His disciples in Matthew 10, Jesus encouraged them to take up their cross, a despicable symbol of torture and thievery. He tells His disciples that he who has found his life will lose it and he who has lost his life, for Jesus' sake, will find it.

Brad

◻   **How do we dethrone the selfish part of ourselves?**

◻   **How well do you understand the perfect and eternal qualities of your redemption?**

◻   **Do you live more often as your true self or as your false one? Why?**

THE FALSE VERSUS THE AUTHENTIC

"The ego is the false self born out of
fear and defensiveness."

— JOHN O'DONOHUE

| 2 Corinthians 5:17 | Isaiah 57: 9-10 | Romans 6:4 |

We place ourselves at the center of the universe. God removes us and takes the spot for Himself. Such is God's order of the universe. When we understand this, we find our true state of being. Man believes that life starts at birth. God believes that life starts at death. Each day we attempt to deny the self, the id of our lives, according to Sigmund Freud.

Paul wrote that we have been "raised up with Christ" (Ephesians 2:6). He's referring to being raised up on a cross. Indeed, he is saying that we have died with Jesus, and we should seek the higher things because that's where Jesus is, at the right hand of God. Paul exhorts us to set our minds on heavenly things because that is where our true life is hidden. He also reminds us that when Christ is revealed, our true selves will also be revealed with Him in glory (Colossians 3:1-4).

Can you imagine? Jesus will share His glory with us, and the Father will see us as perfect people, created in His image.

We must walk the tightrope of these two realities: We are fallen, yet we have been made perfect. Each one of us has been remade into an image of our Father God.

One way to think about our self is to evaluate whether we are net givers or net takers. It has been said that takers eat well, but givers sleep well. Indeed, we were made to be instruments of love. We have been remade as temples of the living God with Jesus Himself residing in our heart. And if God is in our heart, we will live to give real life to others.

When we forfeit our soul, it's not just one exchange. It is a thousand small exchanges as we stumble through life. We don't discover our soul in one exchange but in a thousand small transactions of love.

Isn't that really what we desire in the core of our being? We want to find our authentic life. We don't want to live other people's lives or imitate some sort of man-made value system. No, we want to understand our own unique gifts, abilities, experiences, friends, teachers, and thoughts. And this unique self is perfect and hidden with Jesus in the heavenlies.

As Thomas à Kempis wrote, "Embrace the holy timbre," and we will discover life on another level.

Brad

———————◆———————

- How do you fit into God's order?

- What does it mean to "take up your cross"?

- How do we understand our fallen nature? Our heavenly one?

DAY 42

ROCKY JESUS

"To follow Christ means to learn the art of life. And the whole curriculum lies in the words, 'Learn of me.'"

— UNKNOWN

| Hebrews 12:29 | Revelation 1:13-16 | Revelation 19:11-16 |

If I were to buy the idea of Jesus sold to me by pop culture—the Sunday school portrait of a finely groomed man in a soft white robe holding a lamb, teaching only the Golden Rule—I'd have a mix of the Snuggle bear, an Irish Spring shepherd and a proto-hippie. Yet this limits Him so much. He is, says and does more.

His explanations of life cause us to wonder where gentle Jesus originated. Read: Luke 6:20-38; Luke 9:23-24; Luke 10:16; Luke 11:23; Luke 12:49-53. Luke 13:24-30; Luke 14:25-33; Luke 19:11-27. These are just a few, and from only one of the four Gospels. We could continue.

This Jesus offers us little room to think He's just a feel-good guru. He's teaching us something deep, hard, and real. And He teaches in ways that are deep, hard, and real. No matter how we understand these words of His, let us at least understand that He communicates something strong. He offers nothing cheap, easy, or convenient.

What do we do? Fyodor Dostoevsky's novel *The Brothers Karamazov* depicts what we've done. "Why hast Thou come to hinder us?" the Grand Inquisitor asks Jesus. "Don't come back," he says, in essence. "You'll ruin everything with your hard sayings. We need to make them less than they are."

Even modern theologians like to play theological twister with Jesus' teachings, contorting His words to something that doesn't stand up under real pressure. Some of His words sound too harsh to take at face value, so we give them a different meaning, one that asks less of us.

Steve Chalke, author of *The Lost Message of Jesus*, recounts a scene from the film, *Gandhi* in which a minister, Rev. Charlie Andrews, walks with Gandhi through a street on which young men threaten them. When Andrews suggests they face potential physical violence, Gandhi responds:

"Doesn't the New Testament say, 'If your enemy strikes you on the right cheek, offer him your left'?"

Andrew replies, "I think perhaps the phrase was used metaphorically."

"I am not so sure," Gandhi counters. "I have thought about it a great deal, and I suspect Jesus meant that you must show courage. Be willing to take a blow, several blows, to show that you will not strike back, nor will you be turned aside... it calls on something... that makes his hatred for you decrease and his respect increase. I think Jesus grasped that, and I have seen it work."

Gandhi understood that Jesus' teachings were neither easy nor dismissible. They required action.

We can accept a pseudo-rabbi-carpenter-teacher-redeemer and pseudo-teachings, but if we do, we will miss Jesus himself. We'll miss the offer of life on the strictest yet most generous of terms: "Give up what you think is life but know is not, and I'll give you everything that is life in return."

When the disciple John put his head on Jesus' chest at the Last Supper, he did not find a soft man. He found a strong man, rigid in a way, demanding, but even more generous in his offer.

He is a rocky man, a man of points and edges and hard surfaces. If we come up against the real man, it'll break us. And then the tender Jesus, as oversimplified by the fashioners of the pop-culture Jesus, can receive us. And with this fierce, unrelenting, strong, and even rocky love, He restores and teaches us, making us new.

Adam

◻ **Do you try to explain away the hard teachings of Jesus? Which ones?**

◻ **How do you reconcile them with the gentle teacher?**

◻ **Why do some of Jesus' words make us uncomfortable?**

EARTH REVOLVES AROUND WHOM?

"Most people are far too much occupied with themselves to be malicious."

— FRIEDRICH NIETZSCHE

| Matthew 6:25-34 | Philippians 4:6-7 | 1 Peter 5:6-8 |

"Are you ever hurt, Dad?" Carol asked.

The question stumped him. A dozen hurts raced through his mind, but none came out.

"Of course, he gets hurt," the wife shot back.

How (and why) do macho men conceal our hurt? Should we wear it more visibly?

These are questions I find difficult to answer. But at the root of this thought is a much more powerful question: "Is our heavenly Father ever hurt?" Or, more pointedly, "How do I hurt Him?"

In the bestselling book *The Purpose Driven Life*, author Rick Warren asserts that, "It's not about you." But our entire existence is one of self-reflection. "How do I look?" "How did I come off in that situation?" "Does this person like me?" "Can I compete with him?"

The question is, how can we rise above this complete self-centeredness into the spirit of self-sacrificing love?

This process drives us mad and starts in our infancy.

In most healthy families, we learn about unconditional love from our parents. They feed us, change our diapers, comfort us, pamper us, hug us, and adore us to the core. These things bring us alive and make us feel loved and protected. We bear our family name and get our identity from it. It's totally about me.

Then brothers and sisters arrive. We must share the stage. We fight them. They fight back. We are punished for our selfishness and told to get along. We must learn to apologize, to say we were wrong, and to reconcile. In this struggle, we realize that the family is stuck together. But it's still about me.

We realize that our family will disappoint us, so we go fishing for friends. These friends look good on the outside, so we decide that we can love them. In the end, we find that these friends are just like our family. Disillusionment sets in. *How can I have meaningful relationships?* It's still about me.

Out of the blue comes a member of the opposite sex. Wow! Our heart pumps and hormones rage. We find ourselves buying flowers, writing notes, and feeling terribly illogical. This isn't necessarily love at all. For some of us, it's just lust. Yet we pursue it nonetheless. We begin to become a different person.

Our values change. And when it's all said and done, most of us are nursing a broken heart. That's when it's really about us.

Eventually we marry. We yearn for love and fulfillment from this life partner. We believe we have security in this relationship, so this time we'll find love and meaning. We raise our expectations and try to derive meaning from marriage. But this too disappoints. And we're left with ourselves.

We have children. Here we learn to shed some of our selfish impulses. We lay down our lives for the children, and this feels very natural. All too often, we live vicariously through them and build high expectations for their lives. Much higher than for ourselves. It's still about us.

In every relationship, God waits for us. After forty years or more, we realize more deeply that He's been there, that He's faithful. He just wants us to love Him—and to display this love in our treatment of others. Each type of relationship becomes its own classroom, each setback its own set of lessons. Eventually we discover that it's all about Him. Some of us learn sooner, some later. Some of us learn the lesson more deeply. But we all discover that this life is really all about Him.

Brad

- How close are you to this discovery that it's all about God?

- What about yourself are you most concerned with?

- Regardless of actual age, what stage of life are you in?

HOMESICK

"If I find myself a desire that nothing in this world
can satisfy it must mean that I was made for
another world."

— C.S. LEWIS

| 2 Corinthians 5 | John 14:1-14 | Luke 15:11-32 |

Returning from vacation, on my way home I drive down familiar roads, knowing the exact location of sharp turns and potholes. I know when to accelerate and just how to brake around the last turn. I pull into the garage and unload. When I open the door to the house, it creaks recognizably. The familiar smell arouses my senses.

I understand this place. I walk the darkened hallways at night, knowing the number of stairs to the top and the location of the end table. I knocked my knee into it far too often. I need no light. I am home.

Beyond these tangibles, home carries the familiarity of people and identity: the sound of Dad grinding coffee beans in the early morning, unmandated gatherings in the living room, and a host of other memories. At home we rest our bodies and souls. We find solace in the familiar, unchanging nature.

What is home? A place? People? Friends? Family? Identity? Yes. But it is also something more, something that eludes description.

Wikipedia offers the paltry definition of a dwelling place for its entry on *home*. It then provides the picture of a house. But a house fails to fully describe a home. Wikipedia knows this, and therefore attempts to supplement the incomplete with popular sayings about the concept: "Home is where the heart is." "There's no place like home." "Home sweet home."

We return to the initial question: What is home? And why do we so desperately want to go there?

In *The Odyssey*, Homer weaves the tale of Odysseus, a brave soldier returning to his homeland, Ithaca, after the ten-year Trojan War. On his journey he encounters enemies, mortal and immortal, that attempt to prevent his homecoming.

Calypso, a seductive goddess, traps Odysseus on her island indefinitely with the allure of endless passion and paradise. Odysseus, the weathered fighter, cries wrenching tears every day. Even in bliss he just wants to go home. Palm trees and lusty nights fail to fulfill that unfulfilled longing.

Calypso questions him. "Is your wife superior to me in stature or beauty?"

"No," he assures her. "You, Calypso, are superior in every way

She questions his reasonings again. All Odysseus can offer is that he wants to go home because he wants to go home.

I want to go home because I miss home. And I know that this world is not it.

Is it possible to miss somewhere I have never been? Does my longing indicate an existence even if I cannot fully explain it? Must I look past the tangible elements that attempt to distract in order to see the intangible promise of home?

Amy

———————◆———————

◻ **What is home?**

◻ **Why do you want to get there?**

◻ **What distractions prevent you from wanting more?**

DAY 45

THE TRICK TO LIFE

"When I get honest with myself,
I admit that I am a bundle of paradoxes."

— BRENNAN MANNING

| Psalm 139:13-16 | Isaiah 43:1-7 | John 15:14-15 |

"The trick to life: You must stop trying to be something and just be what you are and love it." Thus reads the inspirational scrawling on the paper towel dispenser in my favorite café's men's room. The handwriting and adolescent angst indicate the work of a teenager.

Obviously, someone grew tired of the endless struggle to meet a nebulous cultural expectation about appearance, attitude, activities, and general persona. He decided to stick with what he'd begun. He'd let the rest sort itself out because any other way would involve too much soul contortionism. "To thine own self be true" he'd heard somewhere, and now he was offering his own twist on the classic line.

It's exceedingly difficult for us to be what we are because we have no clue what that means. Who knows who and what they are? At what point in the educational process or in your parents' tutelage did someone tell you, "Discover who and what you are"? Certainly, you heard, "What do you want to be?" and "What do you want to do?" from age three until those unguided post-college years. Meanwhile you've run after numerous rainbows with pots of career gold at the end, hoping to stave off questions about your contributions to society and your 401(k). But no one taught you to ask yourself, "Who am I?" How could you know?

Perhaps you can know something: you're a son or a daughter, a brother or a sister or an only child; you're a friend, a father, a mother, a husband, a wife; you're a clerk, an attorney, a student, a teacher, a salesman, a waitress. These are all roles you play, but do any of these roles really tell you who and what you are? Do these begin to touch on your essence, your deeper personality, your spirit, your unique make up? After all, everyone plays these roles.

Roles don't answer the question Who am I?

Even if you did ask these questions of identity, how do you find the answers? What criteria do you apply? What authority confers value, meaning, identity upon you? We have plenty of teachers and professors instructing us on everything from astrophysics to zoology, but few teach us how to discover who we are. This precious information eludes us.

Let's look at what the Teacher did. How did Jesus understand Himself, His identity? Jesus found His identity in His Father, as John chapters 5-10 make so clear. He continued to draw strength and clarity in His connection to the Father. He cared only for how His Father saw Him. He knew He was His Father's Son. He then lived accordingly.

If you want to follow Jesus, and to see to know your authentic self, you should heed Jesus' example. Looking to the Father, we can know the answer to the question Who am I?

---◆---

◻ **What does John 14:10-14 say about Jesus' identity?**

◻ **What does it say about the identity of Jesus' followers?**

◻ **Who are you?**

PRUNING

"Sweet flowers are slow and weeds make haste."

— WILLIAM SHAKESPEARE

| Luke 13:6-9 | John 15:1-11 | Hebrews 12:7-13 |

Jesus spoke about pruning. He explained that God prunes His people so they will bear more fruit. Agricultural experts at Texas A&M say that pruning has four purposes: plant health and growth, increased fruit and flower production, safety of people and property, and appearances and aesthetics. What does this mean for us?

Pruning involves cutting and trimming. Cutting off a branch at its joint, figuratively or literally, equals a definite act of severance. That doesn't sound appealing at all.

Let's consider pruning in relational terms.

Some relationships simply take life and never offer it. They fail to build up either party. They're space fillers. In the garden of Eden God gave Adam and Eve to one another for something more than just killing time. He offered life through relationships that met needs that instilled individuals with a sense of communion, purpose, joy, and fulfillment.

God had in mind more than filling space. He intended to fill hearts.

Do all relationships involve some aspect of our heart? Or do some just exist in a vegetative state? Do we have the courage to consider that some relationships may have no momentum to go anywhere? Do we have the audacity to consider pruning those?

Some relationships are dead weight. They appear lifeless because, well, they are. Some people just don't want to be bothered with greater depth. Perhaps such relationships merit pruning. Do we really need more people in our lives with whom we have no real contact? Don't we need more from each other and no more others?

Henry David Thoreau said, "It is not enough to be busy. So are the ants. The question is: What are we busy about? Are we busy going from one dead-end relationship to another? Or are we busy going deeper with a few people we know, who know us? Are we busy giving and receiving life or just watching it pass by?

Does this mean the Spirit can't show up in places that appear untouchable? No. Does this mean that the Lord does not work in something that doesn't bear fruit right away? No. Some seasons are seemingly barren. Perhaps this means that we need a little focus on our relationships, say a little prayer about them. Are they a waste of time? Will they grow?

The outcome of such pruning, of such cutting in our life, if we're to listen to Jesus and the Aggies of A&M, is greater health and growth in our life. We can also expect greater production of fruit. Healthier relationships will certainly translate to lives that are safer for others. And the appearance of life, with greater focus, more simplicity, more growth, would possess more beauty.

It seems so counterintuitive that to grow more, we must cut. To foster growth, we must facilitate a personal severing. Yet such is the way of growth; it comes at a painful price first. Jesus and nature both teach us this, and neither apologizes.

Jesus offers more in life. The offer of more life is on the table. The price involves sacrifice.

Adam

- ☐ **What relationships might you need to prune?**
- ☐ **How might your relationship to the Lord grow through such pruning?**
- ☐ **How might you grow through such pruning?**

REVOLUTION, PROPERLY RECEIVED

"Did you miss me while you were looking for yourself
out there?"

— TRAIN, "DROPS OF JUPITER"

| Luke 12:22-31 | Matthew 16:24-28on | Matthew 26:36-46 |

W e discovered that the earth revolves around the sun—a true revolution of thought. Before that the proponents of such preposterous thinking found themselves excommunicated, officially ostracized by the church. Copernicus and Galileo paid a hefty price for correcting the larger world's self-centered understanding of the universe.

Looking down on that time from our scientific mountaintop, we see irony in the treatment of these men. They revealed truth, right? Why such enmity toward them?

But how much has really changed? Copernicus and Galileo merely hoped to point out that despite apparent signs to the obvious, the earth did not sit at the universe's center. Whenever someone attempts to point out a blemish in my life, I reject the claim, slander the individual, and continue on in my higher view of myself .

Thomas Kuhn explained in *The Structure of Scientific Revolutions* that paradigms do not immediately shift when confronted with contrary evidence. People promoting problematic data challenging the established worldview usually find themselves excluded rather than considered. Do I not do the same to others when their beliefs don't square with mine, specifically the one about my centrality?

From birth I've believed the world revolved around me. I would never come out and say it, yet I live as though it were true. A witness could testify to as much. As a child, I was fed, clothed, bathed, and cared for by others. When I cried, they came running. When I messed myself, they cleaned it up.

As time passed, I grew shrewd in keeping others in my orbit, throwing various fits when I didn't get my way. Hearing no frustrates me to this day; I neither expect nor enjoy this response.

But to understand the universe and my place in it, I need proper perspective. The stars may appear to move around us in circles, but in fact we move while they remain stationary. So is it with God. I revolve around Him, despite my desires to have Him bend to my will like Aladdin's genie.

My desires and perspectives matter little when it comes to God's place, and if I cannot rightly understand His place, I'll face frustration when life steers off script.

Adam

▢   Around what does your life revolve?

▢   How does Jesus understand life's center? (Read Matthew 23:9; Matthew 26:39; Matthew 26:42; Luke 11:12; John 5:19; John 5:30; John 8:28.)

▢   Would you try to put God before yourself? Why or why not?

DAY 48

BURDENS

"I need help with me."

— ANNE LAMOTT

| Galatians 6:1-5 | Matthew 11:27-30 | Psalm 68:19 |

"Dad," he said, "I've had the best week of my life."

Impossible, the father thought. *He's been at a work camp all week. What's he been doing that he enjoyed it? What's been so great?*

"We've worked and been busy, and I haven't thought about myself once. I think that is why I've had so much fun."

We live in a *me* world. Commercialism caters to the individual and builds up the great *me*. A collection of magazine ads reveals as much: "Quench your thirst." "We can get you there." "Is it in you?" "Drive your way." "Where do you want to be?" "Get the good stuff." "An army of one." "Be all you can be." "Your way, right away."

Perhaps all this attention has made us ill. It's one thing to know yourself, and it's one thing to have self-awareness, but we've slipped into self-obsession.

Could this be the reason for the increase in service programs in education? Have we taught our young people to think about themselves so much that we now have to teach them to think of others?

What a chore to think only of ourselves. We grow paralyzed thinking of ourselves. Every morning we clothe ourselves with the burdens of our past, our self-consciousness, and it weighs us down. Our own burden is the hardest to bear, and it binds us, preventing us from thinking of much else. I look in the mirror so often I have no time or energy to look elsewhere.

Then Jesus comes, offering to restore movement to our limp limbs.

"If you'll quit thinking about yourself, you'll have freedom," He admonishes. "But you'll need to stay focused against the world's catcalls, so look at me. Do what I do. Go where I go. Think like I think, and love as I love. The act of forgetting yourself sets you free."

He says, "Come to Me, all who are weary and heavy-laden, and I will give you rest. Take My yoke upon you and learn from Me, for I am gentle and humble in heart, and you will find rest for your souls. For My yoke is easy and My burden is light" (Matthew 11:28-30).

Weary and heavy-laden describes the posture of my soul. Rest sounds so satisfying, and I long for a lighter burden. No one else offers this. The world offers more me and more speed, and neither of those have filled me up. They've only weighed me down. Through centuries of fads and trends, Jesus has persisted. I'll take his burden and let go of mine.

Adam

- ❑ How often do you think of yourself?

- ❑ Do you enjoy it, or does it feel oppressive and binding?

- ❑ What would you like to be free to think of, to focus on instead?

PASSING ON?

"No one on his deathbed
looked up into the eyes of friends and family and said,
'I wish I'd spent more time at the office."

— PAUL TSONGAS

1 Corinthians 15:50-58	1 Corinthians 1:26-31	1 Corinthians 3:10-15

Few people focus on making money in their latter days. In their twilight years, people rarely boast of achievements or primp their appearance . They don't usually lord their authority over others. People nearing the end tend to deal with the questions within.

As people near death their thoughts turn to something higher than themselves. The old ways fall to the side as eyes start searching for meaning, identity, and purpose.

Why?

Perhaps previous distractions become opaque in our later days. Formerly marginal issues move to the center.

Does the end allow for greater receptivity to what didn't produce wealth or beauty or fame? The great distraction, self, with its attendant demands of vanity, greed, and lust, falls away. Why gain more money when you can't spend it? Why try to attain the beauty only youth can claim? Why boast of a life nearing its end?

The decline of the self's pervasiveness opens a great vacuum. It is so great, only some idea or person as big as God can fill it. Only eternal ideas like love and family and friendship and purpose and meaning provide rest for worried souls.

This takes place near our end. Not for everyone, but for many. Space opens inside for God to enter or Jesus to teach. But could it happen in our earlier days? Could we, you and I, learn to focus on His ideas now?

Yes and no. Yes, because there is a way, and no because the self cannot survive the experience. When we choose God, we choose against ourselves. We want to focus on ourselves. But Jesus, the one who spoke of God with such familiarity and authority, says we should watch for and follow God instead. This means neglecting self, ignoring its clamorous cries.

Agony approaches as the self dies slowly, but as we decrease, He increases. We start to live because He is life.

The self will pass away. God has always been, always will be. If I want to live, I can wait for time to pull down the pillars of the world's wealth, or I can begin forgetting the world's ways and its focus on me.

- ◻ How much do you think about yourself?

- ◻ What would you rather focus on?

- ◻ What needs to happen in order to focus more on Him?

REWRITING THE HARD DRIVE

"I saw the angel in the marble and carved
until I set him free."

— MICHELANGELO

| Romans 12:1-8 | Isaiah 55:6-11 | Psalm 119:9-16 |

Wanting to do some more writing, I looked for a laptop. Pen and paper can't compare to a word processor for speed and easy storage. My friend knew this, and he came up with a free used IBM his nephew was getting rid of. It seemed like an answer to a prayer. Then I pushed the power button.

The machine for which I paid nothing appeared to be worth the cost. It wasn't loaded with Microsoft Word. The old files needed deleting, and the operating systems moved slowly. I had to download a great deal of software to even begin doing anything.

Jesus said believing is the work of God. My friend thinks he means we are like computers. We need to clean up the old files, rework our operating systems, and download new software.

To believe in Jesus feels entirely out of the ordinary, completely beyond our comfort zone, and like a logical impasse. Look at what Jesus promises. Read His teachings and see if you believe Him. The gospels brim over with bold and preposterous claims, and these claims don't function with my mind's operating system.

Keep reading what he says. His Sermon on the Mount confounds my value and judgment systems. Blessed are the poor? Turn the other cheek? Looking at a woman lustfully equals adultery? Love my … enemies? Jesus' words seem more like fantasy and idealism at best. Neither of these relate to my mind's programs of realism, cynicism and empiricism.

Following Jesus and believing Him entails a complete rewrite of my mental, spiritual, and emotional hard drives. Most of what lives within me conflicts with His words.

He keeps telling me, "You've heard it said, but I tell you" as if to point out that my hard drive needs a clean sweep. His words need to take the place of my current operating system.

I need much work. Therefore, downloading His thinking and ways of acting proves terribly difficult. It requires daily efforts and deposits of time. Each choice I make needs to run through the new system. Believing that the effort is worth it, and believing in His words, are the work He gives me. It means not just hearing the words but putting them into practice.

▢   Which of your thoughts conflict with Jesus'?

▢   What efforts are you making to compare your thinking
     with His?

▢   What one teaching of Jesus bothers you the most?
     Why? What are you doing about it?

ABSENCE OF ARISTOCRACY

"Every marriage tends to consist of an aristocrat
and a peasant, of a teacher and a learner."

— JOHN UPDIKE

| John 18:28-40 | John 12:12-19 | 1 Samuel 8:10-22 |

Jesus said that He's a king. The writers of the Hebrew Scriptures refer to God as a king and assert that He understands Himself as such.

This compares to reading Dr. Seuss for me. A collapsible frink, a dawf, or a foona-lagoona baboona is like a king to me: I'd know it only if someone pointed it out. I'm American. We're all equal in our eyes. Thomas Jefferson put it on paper, and those who think their blood is bluer look like fools to us.

In the West, we're so equal that we become provincial authorities.

"Who are you to instruct me? We're equal," we think. Sadly, this thought process bleeds into my relationship with Jesus.

He says, "I'm a king."

I respond, "What's a king? Some strange, ancient feudal title? We're American; we're all the same."

Yet how can I properly approach someone whose position I contend with, ignore, or don't understand? Try to imagine a student not recognizing the authority of his teacher, a private ignoring a lieutenant colonel's directives, a paralegal dismissing a partner's request for assistance. The issue involves position and authority.

He asks me to let Him lead. He asks no small thing. I hail from the institution of the individual, where I blaze my own trails to mark my significance.

Can I approach God through Jesus if I won't see the king's crown? I certainly cannot view Him as an impeachable elected official swayed by polls, despite my desires. He really is above me, and He expects that I see this and defer to it.

If I refuse, I'll certainly miss the point of God desiring to come be with me, to dine and talk and share experience.

I'll miss the significance of Jesus' words: "No longer do I call you slaves, for the slave does not know what his master is doing; but I have called you friends" (John 15:15).

He waits. He knows my stubbornness, my insolence, and He gently works out the knots that keep my neck bowed. He allows me to view Him as a friend for the moment. Yet He knows that a time approaches when I'll gawk at the love of the billionaire because He'd walk with me, a pauper.

I'll realize who calls me a friend.

Adam

————— ◆ —————

- ❑ What's an example of royalty in your world?

- ❑ Does it strike you at all as magnificent?

- ❑ How can you understand who God is if you don't understand the significance of a king?

GOD BEFORE
OTHERS

DAY 52

FAMILY FIRST

"The true soldier fights not because he hates what is in front of him, but because he loves what is behind him."

— G.K. CHESTERTON

Luke 14:26	1 John 4:20	1 John 3:15

"I hate you!" my little brother wailed as we stood on the edge of our grandparents' pool, staring down at the shiny, precious thing he wanted so badly for Christmas. His shiny new, remote-controlled monster truck lay on the tiled bottom.

Thankfully, my mother stepped in to shield me from his rage. He was told to forgive me because I was his sister. For all our flaws, love of family (or at least absence of hatred) was a bedrock component of our childhood home.

Family values are such a strong, vibrant thread in our nation's moral fiber that politicians often posture about being a "family-first" candidate. Corporations make a point to market their products as being family friendly. A positive emphasis on family has become a cultural value, and a seemingly universal good.

Unlike the consumer and voter, Jesus doesn't buy in. Despite His kindness to people and children, He held no special regard for blood relatives. Jesus directed His disciples to leave behind parents and siblings and even hate them as they follow Him. The accounts of His life on earth chronicle this puzzling pattern over and over.

His subversive stance on family seems shocking. The Bible is so chock-full of exhortations to love all beings—God, our neighbor, the leper, the foreigner, the enemy—that we balk when Jesus throws out the word "hate." Hate our brother? The same one you asked us to lay down our life for a few verses ago? What's the deal?

Language barriers sometimes skew our English understanding of what Jesus is asking us to do. *Miseo*, the Greek word for hate, is seen throughout the Bible and means "loved less than."

Jacob *loved* his second wife Rachel but *hated* Leah in comparison. Likewise, Jesus wants us to love God so much that by comparison the love we have for our families looks like indifference. His miracles drew great crowds, and so He challenged them with a description of the cost of following Him: preferring Him above all else, even kin.

Hollis

---◆---

◻ In what ways are faith and family incompatible?

◻ When has your faith pitted you against your family?

◻ Does the instruction to hate tramp upon the commandment to love?

DAY 53

INSULT AND INJURY

"Blessed are you when people insult you and persecute you, and falsely say all kinds of evil against you because of Me. Rejoice and be glad, for your reward in heaven is great; for in the same way they persecuted the prophets who were before you."

— MATTHEW 5:11-12

| 2 Corinthians 5:17-20 | Ephesians 4:20-24 | Galatians 2:20 |

We bear inherent risks when we seek to please our heavenly Father. Pleasing Him will inevitably lead to conflict with those whom we would rather please—our friends and colleagues. How many times has God called us to take actions that look strange to worldly observers?

If God asks me to spend extra time with Him some morning and I do, I may be late for work. In my job I am allowed such flexibility, but those around me may think I'm lazy. Then they might talk about me. Indeed, they may discredit me, make fun

161

of me, and insult me, but I am just being obedient to Jesus. In my flesh I greatly fear these things.

How subtle is the temptation to worry about pleasing people, even when such an act conflicts with pleasing the one to whom we must give an account. He is the only one we need to please.

If there is persecution, make sure it's because of Jesus and not because of some human whim or act of pride. We know in our hearts whether our stand is for Him or for ourselves. And the adversary would love to trip us up here.

But Jesus takes it to a deeper level in the beatitudes. In the face of opposition, He says, "Rejoice and be glad, for your reward in heaven is great; for in the same way they persecuted the prophets who were before you" (Matthew 5:12).

Rejoice and be glad? How can we? We have been reviled, slandered, rejected by people who feel more real than things unseen.

Why not respond with holy retribution? Because the only One who deserved to respond in such a way chose not to. He chose love. He chose to forgive. He chose to rejoice in the victory of His death and resurrection. And to leave justice to the only one deserving of carrying out justice: our Holy Father.

When we dwell on these things, can we truly live with divine perspective?

The Holy Spirit reminds us constantly: "The Lord sustains all who fall and raises up all who are bowed down" (Psalm 145:14).

Brad

- What lie are you most concerned with others believing about you?

- What pieces of your identity do you need to release in order to follow God's promptings?

- Whose approval means the most to you?

THE GOOD, THE BAD AND THE IMMATERIAL

"If you are here to help me, you have come for the wrong reasons, but if you are here because your liberation is directly bound in mine, then come walk beside me and we can find hope together."

— JESUIT VOLUNTEER MOTTO

Matthew 15:15-20	2 Timothy 4:3	Matthew 19:16-19

A little girl rode shotgun as her father drove to the grocery store. Opening the glove compartment, she discovered a pack of Marlboro Lights.

"Whose are these?!" she screamed in disbelief and disgust.

Her father calmly looked at the cigarettes and then at this daughter. "They're mine," he said.

Her eyes grew wide, and she gasped, "You're going to hell!"

The man, startled, immediately pulled over the car. He had not taught her such things, and they didn't attend church, so he was at a loss to the origin of this doctrine. He then turned to her and asked, "Who told you that?"

"Everyone knows it," she responded with conviction.

As a scholar of the Scriptures, he told her clearly, "Sweetheart, let me tell you something. People don't go to hell for smoking or drinking or cursing. I can see only one reason in the Scriptures that people go to hell, and that's for hating other people. That's it."

He calmly pulled the car back onto the road and proceeded to the grocery. His little girl learned that our firmly held beliefs had come un-tethered from truth.

This same man told my friend she should start smoking not because the prospect of lung cancer is so fantastic, but because smokers know how to hang out with each other and talk. Smoking opens the realm of the imperfect people who have stopped pretending. It allows for conversation because the religious vibe has successfully been annihilated.

Another friend put it this way: "When two people sit at a table and they each have a beer, a certain honesty shows up because it is difficult to maintain a shiny, self-righteous veneer with a Miller Lite in your hand. Some of the best talks I've had about Jesus have been over a beer."

Neither individual would advocate smoking or drinking just to do it. Both men see a cigar or a Camel or a Bud as a relational tool, and one that strips a false veneer and enables honesty.

To smoke or not to smoke is not the question. Nor is it whether to imbibe or not to imbibe. Rather, the question is "What makes us good? What is the conduct the Lord finds pleasing?"

We can easily see what people deem "good." Almost everyone considers Abraham Lincoln and Mother Teresa to be good. But we also consider those who don't drink or smoke to be a little better than others. Why? Is peak physical health a moral virtue? If so, do we properly esteem those who don't indulge in sweets?

No. Because we've concocted a moral cocktail, pouring from various bottles of religious, cultural, and political traditions to fashion something palatable. So what suits God's taste?

Amy

- □ **How do you determine what is good and bad?**

- □ **Why do you do so?**

- □ **How can you align your views more closely to the Lord's?**

GLORY WHORES

"Man lives by affirmation even more than he does by bread."

— VICTOR HUGO, LES MISERABLES

| Galatians 1:10 | Acts 5:2-32 | John 12:37-50 |

I hate wedding receptions. I feel awkward because people won't come right out and tell me how great I am. They won't tell me how good looking I am, how pleased they are at my presence, or how the party would feel terribly boring without me.

All they'd need to say is, "The bridesmaids are fighting over you."

But they don't say this, I rarely have a date, and I never feel certain about my clothes or my presence. It's rough going.

Yes, I am addicted to acceptance and affirmation. I realize that my affirmation should come from God and that people's adulation is fleeting. Yet I'll be happy if I can get just a wee-bit more praise.

Men and women often serve as glory prostitutes. Yet some people derive their identity from God. This sort of affirmation stands in sharp contrast to shallow human praise. It is more like marriage. In it, we must learn to listen, to trust and to find our security in God.

Sociologist Charles Horton Cooley said we view ourselves through the eyes of others. He called it "the looking-glass self."

We struggle to present ourselves to others to be accepted, affirmed, or adored. We become slaves to our perceptions of how they view us. We toil for the praise of peers in our field, and the people we date. We lean on the accomplishments of our children, our studies, our appearances, and on and on.

What if we looked for God's affirmation? He sees us through a looking glass of compassion and mercy, even delight.

For a moment we believe this view. Occasionally, we feel it. But to believe it—and to put it into action—doesn't come easy. Especially when the goods on the street come so cheap.

Why live a life to please God when men and women and children can praise us so soon, so immediately? We can hear them. We feel their affirmation, even if we do have to work at appearances to keep the praise coming.

Why wait to hear from a God we can't see? Why indeed? Because prostitutes offer something cheap that mimics love for a moment but can't satisfy. Prostitutes don't offer love. Only the lover who offers life can give love.

Adam

◻ Whose affirmation do you seek? Any person in particular? Why?

◻ In what ways do you feel exhausted when thinking about someone's opinion of you?

◻ What do Scriptures say God thinks of us? What pleases Him?

DAY 56

READ IT AGAIN, SAM

"When you love first things first, you'll love second things better."

— C.S. LEWIS

| Genesis 22:1-12 | Luke 9:57-62 | Matthew 10:32-39 |

A former governor and a lobbyist approached a friend of mine, himself an influential citizen. They sought his support for a grassroots lobbying group focused on putting family first.

"And all of this is based on the Bible?" my friend asked.

"Oh, yes," they replied.

"Then how do you interpret this Scripture passage? 'If anyone comes to Me and does not hate his own father and mother and wife and children and brothers and sisters, yes, and even his own life, he cannot be My disciple.'" (Luke 14:26).

The well-intentioned pair racked their brains. Then they admitted that they didn't understand the Scripture. But their cause was good. My friend agreed.

Then there's Abraham. Having received in old age a son, the fulfillment of God's promise, Abraham heard God ask him to sacrifice his son. God even said, "your only son, whom you love" (Genesis 22:2).

Would Abraham choose the gift or the Giver? Where did his commitment lie? At his Lord's feet or in his home? Abraham chose to obey his Lord, and the Lord gave his son back to him.

Jesus said that to follow Him, a person must hate his family. Why isn't this quoted in Sunday school?

The Greek word we translate as "hate" means a measure of love so miniscule by comparison that it hardly exists. Meanwhile, we are to love God with all our heart, soul, mind, and strength. How committed are we to Jesus? Would we walk away from everything if asked? When all is said and done, where does our allegiance lie? To whom do we owe it?

We try to love people with everything within us. We then give God a token of our time. If we reverse the order, we find great love that overflows to others. That's the paradox: when we offer to God what seems unfair and impossible, He gives back. The fishing nets Jesus asked the disciples to drop overflowed when Jesus directed the casting. He had asked them to lay something down, and then he empowered them to take it up again.

We're tempted to prioritize people before God. We may think our family deserves the greatest portion of our love. But our Lord asks that we give up everything to follow Him, even our family.

However, the one who asks us to drop our nets can teach us to take them up again.

Amy

- ◻ What is the difference between affection and commitment?

- ◻ How could your family become an idol in your life, a little god to you?

- ◻ How do you increase your affection for the Lord?

FOR WHOM

"Employment is nature's physician
and is essential to human happiness."

— GALEN

| Ephesians 6:5-8 | Colossians 3:22-24 | Luke 22:39-44 |

We're driven to appear employable. We seek out BAs, internships, MBAs, and JDs. Some of us, however, don't want to work for anyone else. We'd rather set our own hours, own a business, and drive the vision of our workdays. Our options seem to be limited to working for others or working for ourselves. We don't ever have the option to not work; we will work. The question is for whom.

If you follow Jesus, you work for Him. Sure, you may not see His name on your pay stub, and He doesn't send W-2s, but He teaches us that we're in His service when we follow Him. And not just forty hours a week.

It's 24/7.

Our work, then, does not have managers, customers, and clients. The Lord's satisfaction comes first. Wherever we work, however we spend our days, we live in His service, on His clock, on His dime. He's the boss who lays out agendas and the customer whose satisfaction matters most.

So what does that mean?

We work to please the Lord. We live to please the Lord. My time in the office should make Him proud, not necessarily the guy signing my checks. He's not the one I'm following through life.

Furthermore, my life outside the office isn't about appeasing any other boss, whether a friend or teacher or group. My time belongs to the Lord, and He's the one for whom I work, whether I eat, drink, play, rest, or travel. The satisfaction of the others comes as a by-product of satisfying Him.

Mother Teresa once said that Jesus was the only person in the world to her. As a result, every person she met was Jesus. Therefore, when she met the poor, the sick, the hungry or imprisoned, she loved Jesus by loving them; she saw Jesus as her aim and her impetus in all things. She belonged to Him through the cross and her affection. Matthew 25 recounts Jesus' teaching on the sheep and the goats. To those who cared for the hungry, the thirsty, the stranger, the naked, and the imprisoned, he says, "You did this to Me."

Everything is for Him.

Adam

- To what extent do you see yourself as God's employee? His servant?

- How does this impact how you work for your employer?

- How does this impact how you view your life's pursuits?

GOD BEFORE POSSESSIONS

MO' MONEY

"I don't know what they want from me.
It's like the more money we come across,
the more problems we see."

— THE NOTORIOUS B.I.G.

| Matthew 6:24-33 | Ecclesiastes 5:10 | Luke 3:14 |

I received an email today from my friend. He works in money. That's the best way I can say it. If I gave his job title, you might get the wrong impression about his line of work, and that would miss the point. Anyway, my buddy told me one of our other buddies had really been hitting home runs at work lately, making some real jack. A little farther down the road of life, a different friend of mine told me I could make some big cash in *his* line of work—yet another job in money.

After reading his email, I thought about how I'd just adjusted my own monthly financial statements to account for profits and losses. I had friends making more in a month than I do in twelve. And I believe that if I so chose, I could do what they do, and do it well. I don't even need to do it as well, just well enough to break my student debt, pay off my car, and be home each day by 4 p.m. Instead, I work days and a few nights a week, then head to a restaurant to bartend and wait tables—for poor tippers, at that.

No matter how often people with money tell you money won't make you happy, you can't help but think: *Sure. Let's swap places and talk later.*

Jesus said life is more than food and clothes. Money helps, but there's more to life. You, in the back row, I know that you need these to live, but if we're living for these things, don't we miss the point? Aren't there more pressing needs to the big picture of our life?

Maybe Jesus was indicating that life is comprised of dreams, passions, relationships, memories, laughter, love. Food and clothes are good, but when we focus on these it's like going to school and concerning yourself only with whether or not you have papers and books and pens.

Adam

- ◻ **What are the school supplies you're concerning yourself with, causing you to miss the lesson?**
- ◻ **What "one thing" are you waiting for to make you happy?**
- ◻ **How can you value relationships more than material sustenance today?**

THE BETTER BOAST

"Wit beyond measure is man's greatest treasure."

— J.K. ROWLING

| Psalm 139 | Genesis 15 | 1 Corinthians 13:12 |

People are impressed with strength, wisdom, and riches (not to mention beauty, wit, and talent). God is not unless, of course, it is from Him. The things in which God delights are much less visible, much less recognizable, much more difficult to attain, and most important, given very little attention in this life.

> Thus says the LORD, "Let not a wise man boast of his wisdom and let not the mighty man boast of his might, let not a rich man boast of his riches; but let him who boasts boast of this, that he understands and knows Me, that I am the LORD who exercises lovingkindness, justice and righteousness on earth; for I delight in these things," declares the LORD (Jeremiah 9:23-24).

Of all the metrics humans have devised to measure wealth and influence, we have yet to invent a measure of how much a person (a) understands and (b) knows the Lord. Yet understanding and knowing are the boast-worthy qualities mentioned in Jeremiah.

Perhaps our hands are tied by the English translation of those words. "Understand" and "know" may be common to our Western ears, but in Hebrew these words together bear a bit more significance. The Hebrew meaning of *yada*, "to know" (and "understand" in certain contexts), goes beyond mere mental knowledge. *Yada* carries with it the idea of a covenant and was first used in Genesis to describe the intimate relationship of a man to his wife. To know is to be joined in physical and spiritual oneness.

But "knowing" is not limited to the intimate, physical realm of marriage. Treaties, official code for covenants, used *yada* as a way of communicating mutual loyalty from the parties involved in honoring the contract. When God says He "knows" Abraham, it means they are joined in a covenant relationship, one in which mutual loyalty resulted in the nation of Israel.

David says it best: "O LORD, You have searched me and known me... For You formed my inward parts; You wove me in my mother's womb" (Psalm 139:1,13). At the molecular level, we are known and loved by the greatest force in the universe, our Creator. We can run, but we cannot hide.

Adam learned this, Abraham knew this, David knew this, and by understanding the Hebrew origins of the word "know," we can more fully understand what is truly worth boasting about.

When the disciples returned to Jesus after casting out demons, what did He say?

> I saw Satan fall like lightning from heaven. I have given you authority to trample on snakes and scorpions and to overcome all the power of the enemy; nothing will harm you. However, do not rejoice that spirits submit to you, but rejoice that your names are written in heaven. (Luke 10:18-20 NIV)

Hollis

————— ♦ —————

◻ **What do you boast about?**

◻ **To what extent do you understand that the invisible things are of more eternal consequence than the visible?**

◻ **Do you care? Why or why not?**

PYRAMID SCHEMES

"Money. You... you think I want money? What I want is
my morning back. I need you to give my time back to me.
Can you give me back my time? Can you give my time
back to me? Huh? Can you?"

— DOYLE GIPSON, CHANGING LANES

| Deuteronomy 30:15-20 | Matthew 19:29 | Matthew 11:28-30 |

An old friend called to tell me about his new business. He told me about his business mentor and his associates, how people are finally making what they're worth. "You might be able to cash in too," he said.

Translation: pyramid scheme.

Every now and again, someone I know is seduced by the lust of get-rich-quick schemes. Some are more susceptible than others and chase every opportunity that comes along. Without fail, they all involve network marketing, promises of freedom, great wealth, and no real industry competence. Success stories are revealed and track records presented. And all these schemes require money up front. Someone *does* get paid somewhere.

Such schemes always involve talk of living a whole life, being balanced and a good person.

Friends want to find a way to make more money and they try to sell me on their ideas.

No one tries to sell me inner peace, self-control, or self-knowledge.

No one tries to sell me a means of reconciling my fragmented family.

No one tries to sell me simplicity, focus, vision, wisdom.

Perhaps these just aren't marketable concepts.

Give me a pyramid scheme to create more time, more joy, and to find self-awareness. Don't my friends know that I want something more valuable than a get-rich-quick scheme? I'd rather pursue something for which I have some deep need than chase those greenbacks over which others drool.

Perhaps money comes easier than anything of substance because in the end it has less lasting value. No network or pyramid can offer what I really want and need. A financial windfall doesn't overcome loneliness or problems of a broken family. Residual income cannot satisfy, save for a little financial security. At the end of the day, longings for wholeness, a valuable life, redemption, and deep friendships remain with me. Money doesn't meet those needs.

What I need comes in the form of people and experience, not commodities and securities. I want more than they can offer.

I turned down this friend, as I do all quick-payday offers. I'm drawn to Jesus' track record, His bolder offer and more generous terms. I'm throwing in with His offer of an easy yoke and a light burden.

Adam

———— ♦ ————

- ☐ **What do pyramid schemes, corporate-advancement hoaxes, and other short-cut opportunities promise?**

- ☐ **What does Jesus offer?**

- ☐ **Who more accurately meets your needs? Who is more capable of doing so?**

POOR DAD, RICH DAD

"Success in life comes not from holding a good hand,
but in playing a poor hand well."

— DENIS WAITLEY

2 Corinthians 8:1-5	Hebrews 12:2	Luke 21:1-4

In his bestselling book *Rich Dad, Poor Dad*, Robert Kiyosaki shows how you can make more money through income-generating assets. Read: real estate. Kiyosaki claims to teach you how to make money the way his "rich dad" mentor, not his "poor dad" paternal father, taught him.

The rich dad can teach you how to generate income, but can he teach you why you should make it?

Perhaps not. Perhaps the poor dad can, though.

We can learn from everyone. Rich dad can teach you to make money, to invest money. The poor dad teaches you what money is for. Or so he taught me.

I once spent ten days among the very poor in Cuba. My guide, a middle-aged teacher, showed my friend and me his old neighborhood, city, and region. He prepared lavish meals for us, though when we left, he and his family returned to eating one or two simple dishes daily.

Our guide took us to see his friends. A young couple gave us the same treatment, giving generously and asking nothing in return. The wife told us, "We should treat guests like this. We never know when we might entertain angels."

Another man, a farmer, slaughtered one of his lambs to feed us. We ate dinner on the remains of his home, which was swept away by a hurricane. We feasted, sitting on a concrete footprint. That night, this man and his children slept in a 20-foot-by-8-foot shack.

None of these paupers splurge in spending on themselves, but they do splurge on guests. They unload their coffers for friends, visitors, and strangers. Money is like the self. It does the most when it is poured out. As food is for eating and sharing, so money is for using to bless others. The rich dad would have you think that money itself is the point. The poor dad shows you that giving it away, that using it for others, is the point. Hoarding it makes little sense.

They get it. And it humbles the son of the rich dad, for he sees the poverty of his education. He sees the limits of his first-world perspective. He saves his best wines, champagnes, cognacs, and cigars. He doesn't bless his guests this way, especially strangers.

What does Jesus say about the poor? He always tells us to look at them. Perhaps by looking at them we learn from them. We need to learn about values and money. We need to learn to give. These who could most easily worship money due to their lack somehow hold it more loosely; they understand its place more than those with abundance. That's real wealth.

That's the lesson of the poor dad.

Adam

————◆————

- ▢ **What purpose does money play in your life?**
- ▢ **Do you spend time with the poor? Why or why not?**
- ▢ **What are the differences in the education you receive from the wealthy and the poor?**

VESTED INTEREST

"Someone told me that if you'd owned one share of
Coca-Cola stock one hundred years ago, it would've split
one thousand times by this point. No one I know has
held shares of anything for a century,
but you get the point."

— RENE RIVKIN

| 1 Timothy 6:17-21 | Matthew 6:24-34 | Luke 12:13-34 |

Albert Einstein said, "The most powerful force in the universe is compound interest." The longer the interest accumulates, the faster it grows.

What will win me a greater return? Given equal annual yields of a safe five percent, will a thirty-year investment perform better than a hundred-year investment? The latter always dominates the former; the time value involved carries the hundred-year investment to heights the thirty-year couldn't imagine.

But we don't live long enough to reap the rewards of a century's worth of investing, do we? But others could. Our investments could pay out huge annuities to others.

Must long-term investing refer to the IRA you can safely tap? What of investing in others, for others, and not merely your children or children's children? What if we made investments according to God's values? His kingdom desires love, mercy, justice (see Micah 6:6-8), and reconciled lives. The returns on these, while not material , put the savviest fund managers to shame.

Jesus says what we should all honestly recognize, realistically embrace, and pragmatically consider that the world's wealth passes away. Only an investment in a spiritual bank is secure for long-term performance. Only investments in God's proverbial marketplace never burn, corrupt, or pass away.

Consider the following: J. Pierpont Morgan or Mother Teresa? Glenn McCarthy or Martin Luther King Jr.? Dhirubhai Ambani or Mahatma Ghandi? Whose investments will continue to yield results for the sick, the orphaned, civil rights, and India? Whom do we remember?

Let's not say that Morgan, McCarthy and Ambani lived lesser lives, but we clearly see the others living for and investing in what God values. Mother Teresa, Dr. King, and Ghandi invested in an invisible market. The interest continues to compound at amazing rates in the lives of people everywhere.

Whose investment practices do you want to model? Morgan's? Or King's?

Remember the words of Johann Wolfgang von Goethe: "Whatever you can do or dream you can do, begin it. Begin it now."

Adam

————◆————

- ☐ **On what do you spend the currency of your time?**
- ☐ **Who benefits from your investments? Who will tomorrow?**
- ☐ **What reaps the greatest harvest in our lives?**

POSSESSED OF A CAUSE

"Pray that my work for the poor
doesn't get in the way of my love for God."

— MOTHER TERESA, TO ONE WHO ASKED
HOW TO PRAY FOR HER

| Proverbs 3:1-18 | Hebrews 13:5-6 | Matthew 13:22 |

These people always intrigue and sadden me. They have bumper stickers decrying the plight of a people or the earth. They rally and picket. They have a cause (or maybe the cause has them). And they're filled with rabid poison toward their adversaries.

You know them. They show up on twenty-four-hour news channels, in your college classrooms, at protests and political fundraisers. They burn with passion for their cause, supposedly spurred on by love. But you can feel their anger and bitterness.

For such people who lean left, President George W. Bush was a gift. For all the talk of peace and progress, these groups hated this man. He gave them a raison d'être. Hate does little for the group's stated goals.

For those who tilt to the right, ditto Clinton or Obama or Biden (and "liberals" as a group). For all the talk of morality and righteousness, many social conservatives undermine their cause as they emotionally burn the former president in effigy.

Mother Teresa got it. Her cause was caring for the poor and dying in Calcutta. Few people had more reason to yell and scream and grow angry from frustration. The dying and abandoned have few champions, and a capable world turns a blind eye to these inconvenient and uncomfortable people.

Mother Teresa saw that if she clung too tightly to this cause, she'd steal it from the God who gave it to her. She could be tempted to think it was about her, and she'd forget the author of the vision.

Love resurfaces.

Love for God and then others, even our enemies, must come first, before a cause or passion. If it does not, our cause will destroy us. Causes make merciless taskmasters. Whether we lose hope, forget that God calls the shots, or quit seeing our enemies as made in God's image, we'll learn bitterness, cynicism, hate, and anger.

If my heart is full of causes, what do I have to offer a hurting world? If I have passion and resources and a willingness to live and die, but have not love, what am I?

Adam

- What price do you pay within yourselves for a cause?

- What is the ultimate reason for your cause?

- What lies beneath it in you? Anger? Fear? Real love?

THE HOUSE OF STEWARDS

"All of us ought to have some kind of cause,
some kind of purpose in our lives that's bigger than our
own individual hopes, dreams, wants and desires."

— COACH JOE EHRMANN

| Matthew 25:14-30 | Luke 12:13-21 | Luke 12:29-31 |

Jesus tells a parable about people and what they've received. Some Wall Street aficionados might tout this as Jesus' endorsement for capitalism, but we can safely assume the waters run more deeply than economic theory.

A wealthy man gave three of his brokers three different sums of money to manage. Time passes, and he returns, asking each man for an accounting of his investments.

"How have you managed what I gave you?"

How indeed? He could ask this of me. I have money, and though not much by Western standards, it is a great deal compared to the other 99 percent of the world. On what have I spent it? How have I used it? Did I squander it on myself? Have I hoarded it? How much did I give to others?

When we meditate on this parable, we begin to see the message Jesus emphasizes: what you hold doesn't have your name on it. Someone else's name is on it. You merely handle it. You are a steward, sort of like the crazy guy in *The Return of the King*. The throne, while you keep it warm, belongs to someone else.

Am I a steward? The implications of stewardship begin to percolate into my life. God owns everything. Does that include my time, money's fraternal twin? Does His ownership encompass my talents and abilities? And what of my relationships? Do those belong to me or to God?

Let's go back to the parable. The wealthy man in the parable expects profits. Granted, the original story includes a master and servants, not a financier and some fund managers. This guy's proposal included no commissions or fees. One of the servant-brokers even brings this up: these guys bust tail and beat feet to make him the profit.

But the master rewards each in proportion to his handling of the resources received. And the one who complained? His plaintive nature only echoed his deeper nature: laziness and selfishness. He couldn't and wouldn't think of benefiting another, even one whose authority superseded his.

Life lived for self makes for a small story, or one not even worth telling. A life lived for another makes for romance. A life lived for many others can be epic. And life lived for Jesus wins the applause of the great teacher Himself.

Adam

———— ◆ ————

- ¤ What values exist in working and living for yourself?
- ¤ What are you doing for others with what you have?
- ¤ For whom are you making a profit?

DAY 65

STATE OF THE HEART

"For richer or poorer, in sickness and health,
in good times and bad."

— TRADITIONAL MARRIAGE VOWS

| Job 1:20-22 | Mark 12:38-44 | Psalm 37:3-6 |

Talking heads on television tell us how to become wealthy. They tell us about our potential, our destiny, or God's reward for our behavior. Some charlatans or shysters promise a home in the Hamptons and four-car garage. The worst of these peddlers are those who find some obscure scriptural reference to justify how you too can grow filthy rich.

"God wants you to be rich," they thunder or suggest, depending on the audience.

"He promises to bless." This, supposedly, means anyone of sincere faith who believes enough will fall into the highest tax bracket. Eventually.

The real problem with this line of thinking is that it misses what God cares about. Rich or poor, God's concern rests on the condition of a person's heart.

But this doesn't play as well on a larger social psyche. Few of us get geeked up hearing a preacher or cleric shout, "God wants you to love him so much you'll give away all you own! God wants you to love Him more than everyone else in your life!"

Is this not what God wants? The quantity of money the widow gave did not pique Jesus' interest; the proportion to her net worth did. She had little, and of what she had, she gave her all. She wanted to give to God. She wanted to give all of what she had, even if it counted little in our economy.

God cared greatly about how Job responded to Him and to his personal loss.

Throughout Exodus, Leviticus, Numbers, and Deuteronomy, God continued to stress the idea of remembering: Do not forget Him who blesses as you enjoy the blessing. Do not forget with whom you have a relationship.

Where does our commitment lie? With a person or a possession?

What love do we nurture more – our love for God or our lust for wealth and its accompanying status?

God knew from the outset we'd always struggle to love Him and even our neighbors. He knew we would love possessions, so he gave as the last of his commandments the admonition to not covet.

The first commandment? Love God above all else. The last? Don't love things. Remember, He says with the first. Do not forget, He says with the last.

Adam

- ❑ **What commandment(s) hadn't the rich young ruler in Luke 18:18-24 kept?**

- ❑ **How can we gauge what is closest to our hearts?**

- ❑ **What do you find when you take inventory of what you value?**

DAY 66

WHY GIVE?

"None has ever become poor by giving."

— ANNE FRANK

| Exodus 20:17 | Exodus 23:10-12 | Deuteronomy 14:22-15:11 |

Some estimates say the Scriptures mention poverty more than two thousand times. In the city it is on street corners, under bridges, and in alleys at night. Someone needs or wants, and they ask. Or someone needs, which asks something of us.

"You always have the poor with you," Jesus said in John 12:8.

God said, "The poor will never cease to be in the land" (Deuteronomy 15:11). Jesus said, "Give to everyone who asks of you" (Luke 6:30), echoing what God commanded in Deuteronomy 15:11: "You shall freely open your hand to your brother, to your needy and poor in your land." Jesus never said, "Unless you think he'll spend it on alcohol or drugs" or "only if you know he really needs it" or "if you can afford it" or "but if you've tithed you don't have to." He just tells us to give.

Why? We could make the case that Jesus is teaching us to be like Himself in all His teachings. He teaches us to give.

Perhaps He tells us to give so that we interact with those we'd prefer to ignore. This giving connects us to those society forgets.

Perhaps He tells us to give, so we can learn to give. This giving teaches us what God is like: He gives because we need. He gives because we ask. He gives because He loves.

Perhaps He tells us to give, so we might remember that our possessions don't exist for us. This might separate us, even slightly, from loving our goods or money more than we should.

Jesus does not stop with His words. He lives a life exemplifying what He taught. Whatever you see Jesus teach, you'll see Him live. He says, "Forgive," and He forgives. He says, "Reconcile," and He reconciles. He says, "Love," and He loves. He says "Heal," and He heals. He says "Give," and He gives. In the Gospels we see that He gives it all. He gives His life.

"Greater love has no one than this, that one lay down his life for his friends" (John 15:13), Jesus said.

When He tells us to give to the poor, He is teaching us to love. As children crawl before they walk, so we must learn to give our possessions before we can give everything.

Adam

———◆———

- ¤ **Why do you resist giving to the poor? How do you get off the hook?**

- ¤ **Do you give things other than money, like time or affection?**

- ¤ **With what are you unwilling to part? Why can't you give something?**

DAY 67

THINGS I OWN?

"The earth does not belong to us;
we belong to the earth."

— ATTRIBUTED TO CHIEF SEATTLE

| Leviticus 25:23-24 | Psalm 24 | Haggai 2:6-9 |

Think about the things you own. You have clothes, shoes, books, a computer, maybe a laptop, a car, a surfboard and a nifty backpack. A lot of our time goes toward their acquisition and care.

How many resources does it take to purchase and maintain your computer, mountain bike, oriental rug, jewelry, or car? How much do we work to accumulate more goods, or care for the ones we have?

Who possesses whom? Maybe it's not ours after all.

What if it all belonged to God? Our car. Our house. Our land. He owns our boat and our closet of clothes. This stuff doesn't belong to us; it's the Lord's. The documents we call Scripture refer to God's possession of, well, everything.

The psalmist quotes God as saying, "For every animal of the forest is mine, and the cattle on a thousand [read: infinite] hills. I know every bird in the mountains, and the creatures of the field are mine" (Psalm 50:10-11, NIV).

If it all belongs to Him, we needn't worry. If it doesn't belong to us, why bear the anxiety? We can't lose what we don't have.

Should we mistreat what He's put into our hands? Certainly not! That would betray the gift. And besides, it's not ours to abuse. We should care for it without living for it. Better yet, what if we left things better than we found them? The master would appreciate it.

Will the world end if someone steals from us? (And yes, I've been robbed more than once.) No. When we held it, we did not own it; when we hold it no more, nothing has changed.

What can I do if everything belongs to God? I can share. I can give. I can use whatever shack or mansion I inhabit to care about, give to, and entertain others.

I can also be free from believing my net worth rests in perishables. What was I thinking? Now I can think of other matters, matters of real import, like people, relationships, and ideas.

Either my things belong to God, or I belong to my things. We shouldn't fool ourselves into thinking another way exists. Someone owns everything, and it is never we. Nor I.

Adam

———————◆———————

◻ How do your possessions own you?

◻ What are the implications of believing something belongs to God?

◻ If you weren't thinking about your stuff and money, or yourself, what would you think about?

OLD COVENANT,
NEW COVENANT

DIRECTION OF CHANGE

"You make me want to be a better man."

— MELVIN IN AS GOOD AS IT GETS

| 1 Samuel 16:1-13 | Isaiah 29:13-14 | Matthew 23:1-39 |

Do I eat because I am hungry, or do I eat because the clock flips to noon? Am I motivated because of the internal or because of the external? Do I function on body time or by mechanical time?

Russian scientist Ivan Pavlov pioneered experiments testing these psychological motivations, known as classical conditioning. He gave dogs food after ringing a bell. Through repetition he conditioned dogs to associate the sound of the bell with food. When the bell rang, the dogs salivated. After a while the stimulus elicited a reaction whether food was delivered or not. Their minds transformed into formulaic machines: bell equals food.

I am like Pavlov's dogs. I try to reduce a covenant relationship with God to a formula. He calls me to love Him, and I prefer to obey the rules. When will I understand that behavior modification never works?

It manifests external change but fails to cause any internal transformation. It mimics something real but proves to be only a façade. We confuse cause and effect. We attempt to love God by following the rules. God desires for us to love Him and then obedience will naturally follow.

His love does not hinge on our abstinence from drinking, smoking, swearing, or taking part in the myriad of other notably "sinful" activities. He does not desire for us to have good Christian reputations. He wants more. He wants it all. He rejects a polished veneer if the interior is rotten. He is not into appearances. He is concerned with the core.

Pharisees, the publicly religious men of Jesus' times, rejected this apparently heretical statement. They preferred to applaud themselves on their impeccable devotion to rules and achievements of holiness. Jesus destroyed this illusion like a tossed stone disturbs the smoothness of a pond. The ripples erupted in concentric circles. He renounced their hypocrisy, comparing their lives to cups that are washed brilliantly clean on the outside but on the inside remain filthy and unwashed.

Change, true change, emanates from the inside out. It does not work in reverse. A heart change transforms the whole being.

Amy

———— ◆ ————

- What rules do you treat with rigidity?

- How does the inside change?

- How do you live inside out?

OLD COVENANT, NEW COVENANT

"May all your expectations be frustrated.
May all your plans be thwarted. May all your desires be
withered into nothingness, that you may experience
the powerlessness and poverty of a child and sing and
dance in the love of God the Father, the Son,
and the Spirit."

— LARRY HEIN

| Matthew 22:34-46 | Galatians 5:1-26 | Hebrews 8:1-13 |

Life is not fair. Often my mom reminded me of this after returning home from yet another day of childhood injustice.

"I know, I know," I would say, but something inside me craved the fairness I adamantly thought I deserved. It is not fair for everyone, but it should be fair for me, I argued with myself. I want the extra helping, the lucky break, and the extra provision.

I want things I don't deserve. I believed in a simple code: mercy for me; justice for them.

Before Jesus arrived, a relationship with God existed in the strict confines of rules, regulations, and endless quest for fairness. God existed above. He made a promise with his people, and they broke them, constantly. They suffered the consequences, the curses of the rupture. Despite their unfaithfulness, the Lord then gave them blessings as well.

In the old covenant system, people offered sacrifices to compensate for their failings. A strict delineation stood between God and His people. Only priests could talk with God in the temple and only at specified times. God had rules and required a mediator, but men took God's boundaries and added their own regulations. The added rules changed the relationship to one founded on rigidity, judgment, and legalism.

Rules offered guidance in the best ways to live not a pathway to encounter the Lord. But people clung to the rules and forgot the spirit. They believed in a formula: If I do this, then God will bless me. But rules do not produce love or incur freedom.

Then Jesus came as a personal messenger and offered love. He came to offer freedom. He came not to shatter tradition and destroy the rules but to impart love in a way we could understand. He gave love a face. He showed it in His actions. He distributed it with His words. He provided an avenue to a relationship with God.

The one-word commandment to love became something attainable—temporarily, incompletely, selectively. Love is hard. Love never reaches completion. We can always do it more and do it better. For us mortals who crave finish lines and endings, we reject the idea of the continual. Instead, we choose rules and prescriptions that are measurable and quantifiable. Did I lie? Did I cheat? Did I swear? The list is endless. If my value and worthiness is based on the answers to these questions, I miss the point. I reject the freedom of the new covenant and elect the confines of the old. I entangle myself in the web of fairness and regulation. I keep score. What will I do when I realize that the score does not count?

- To what degree are you still living within the confines of the law?

- Why do you resist and invoke the rules of the old covenant?

- What does it look like to live in the new covenant?

WHAT IS A COVENANT?

"Faith would be that God is self-limited utterly by his
creation — a contraction of the scope of his will;
that he bound himself to time and its hazards and haps
as a man would lash himself to a tree for love."

— ANNIE DILLARD

| 1 Thessalonians 5:23-24 | Hebrews 6:13-20 | 2 Peter 1:16-21 |

God created a covenant with a human. And I have absolutely
no idea what that means. What is a covenant? Why would
He create one with me?

Webster defines a "covenant" in theological terms as "an
agreement that brings about a relationship of commitment
between God and His people." But this description still
lacks something. A thesaurus offers the synonyms: contract,
agreement, undertaking, commitment, guarantee, warrant,
pledge, promise. How does this impact me?

How can words define the color yellow or the emotion
sadness? How can they encapsulate sights and emotions and

smells? A friend once told me, "I can't describe what garlic smells like, but I know it when I catch a whiff."

What gives a covenant depth, breadth, and life?

Words hold power. Reading, writing, and speaking are ways we exercise this power. The essence of all human relationships expresses itself in word and in deed. The ancients understood this concept. They comprehended the impact of a mere letter, word, or sentence. They realized that through words, God spoke creation into existence. Scribes labored meticulously to preserve these precious words with perfect accuracy. Errors were not an option.

In modern America, we fail to comprehend the power of words. We devalue and demean them. Through the years, the poignancy lost authority. We speak flippantly. Our truth is relative. We shy away from honesty and confrontation, and instead choose social acceptability. We promise things and do not follow through. We state an arrival time and appear an hour later. We embellish stories and tell little white lies. Our yeses are not yeses. Our nos are not nos. We live in a maybe world of unreliable relativity.

Yet God transcends our fickle nature and insincere promises. He utilizes words and employs them with sincerity, precision, and perfection. He molds them into a holy agreement, calls it a covenant, and invites us to join Him in this intimacy.

How strange a broken, fallible person being invited into a covenant relationship with holiness. Why me? I know my failings. I know my fickle nature. I know I don't follow through. I arrive late, and I entertain selfish motives.

God does not. Somehow, inexplicably so, my imperfection does not deter Him. I cannot even grasp the significance. I relegate and reduce Him to an image I can comprehend. In my attempts to encapsulate Him, I assign Him human characteristics. I think He too will fail to follow through, arrive late, not meet expectations, drop the ball, and be plagued by self-serving motives.

He will not.

And yet He offers me the place in something bigger than an agreement, more personal than a partnership: a covenant.

Amy

———◆———

◻ **Do your words mean anything to you?**

◻ **When you say you'll do something, do you? Why or why not?**

◻ **Can you keep another's confidence?**

IMPLICATIONS OF A COVENANT

"Tell him I'll trade him! Me for her! Tell him!!"

—HAWKEYE IN LAST OF THE MOHICANS

| John 15:10-17 | Mark 14:12-26 | Jeremiah 31:27-34 |

I sat in a wooden pew. Candles lit the altar and illuminated the shadows of the ornately cavernous chapel ceiling. Organs and bagpipes played traditional songs, and a radiant woman dressed in white walked expectantly down the long aisle on the arm of her father, who smiled with both joy and sadness.

Weddings allow us to glimpse the eternal and taste the holy. They reflect with a shimmering truth the promises and prospects to come. We were created to be united, to be joined in love. But the union comes at a price and is sealed with a promise. Two cannot transform into one without a death. In the Old Testament, an animal sacrifice marked the creation of a covenant. The body was divided in half, and the covenant makers walked through the parts to say, "may this happen to me if I break the covenant."

In married life after the toasts are made, the dances danced, and the honeymoon enjoyed, the couple must decipher the meaning of the agreement. To truly fuse two into one, the couple must die to their individual preferences and propensities. They enter a relationship where their world is no longer their own. Personal energies shift toward serving another and loving another more than oneself.

A relationship with Jesus is like a marriage. It is an agreement and a promise based in the ultimate love. Why? Why a covenant? Why a promise? Why a death? Because He loves us. He created us. He wants to be with us. He wants a relationship. A deep relationship.

On the eve of His death, Jesus gathered His twelve disciples to demonstrate the intimacy of this covenant. He broke bread and poured wine. Jesus re-established the Old Testament tradition but made it personal. He offered not an animal, but Himself.

"This is my body which is given for you (Luke 22:19). This is my blood (Mark 14:24). Do this in remembrance of Me" (Luke 22:19).

Amy

————◆————

- What does it mean to die? What does it mean to die to yourself?

- What does it mean that Jesus died?

- What does Jesus' death mean to you?

HISTORY OF A COVENANT

"A covenant made with God should be regarded
not as restrictive but as protective."

— RUSSELL M. NELSON

| Ezekiel 36:22-32 | Deuteronomy 6:4-9 | Romans 13:6-14 |

A muscled arm and calloused hand holds high a knife, sharp and glinting in the afternoon sun. In one quick, steady motion, the arm thrusts downward, and the blade finds its mark on the spine of the lamb. The man guides the knife, from the point of entry down the back of the animal, cutting it in two. Small rivers of blood flow freely, marking the event with a sacred solemnity.

Likewise, the world seems to be divided into halves: black and white, light and dark, left and right. In the Old Testament, we observe the existence of blessings and curses—the results of the adherence to or deviation from a covenant.

Blood marks the gravity of such a covenant, something that hinges on life and death. In Bible times, two men created this form of a promise, deeper than an agreement, by sacrificing an animal. They divided it in half, displaying the halves that compose an ultimate whole. These halves represent the two parties and the two possibilities of outcome, either blessings or curses.

Picture a circle creating a clear delineation of limits. The inside of the circle represents obedience to the terms of the covenant. Inside incurs blessings. Anything outside the boundary represents disobedience, a breaking of the terms of the covenant. Curses.

"In the beginning, God created the heavens and the earth" (Genesis 1:1).

In the beginning, God created, and He created us. He created us to live in relationship, communion, and communication with Him. His covenant terms stem from love. He desires us to know Him and to know how to live. He establishes rules not for the sake of legalism but for a purpose utterly beyond our shortsighted vision. And we broke the covenant. Continually. We chose to dabble and indulge outside the contours of the covenant. And we received the curses. Yet we also received the blessings.

Why? Because God redeems and reconciles all things and all people to Himself. Because He is love. Because He loves us. Because we defiantly choose punishment, and He offers us mercy that originates in true love.

◻   Why would God make a covenant with you?

◻   What do curses and blessings look like? Give examples.

◻   What does it mean for God to reconcile people to
    himself? To you?

FAITHFULNESS

PRESENCE IS REQUESTED

"If you want to avoid worry,
do what Sir William Osler did:
Live in 'day-tight compartments.'
Don't stew about the futures.
Just live each day until bedtime."

— DALE CARNEGIE

| Luke 11:3, 5-13 | John 6:25-35 | Revelation 3:20 |

Looking at the new Bible software on my computer, I came across some of John Wesley's notes. Amazingly, I can look up his or Matthew Henry's famous commentary on almost any passage of Scripture.

Having recently spent time in Luke 11, I searched for Wesley's and Henry's words on the Lord's prayer. Neither of them explicitly made this connection for me, but something in one of the commentaries mentioned that Jesus talks about retrieving bread from a friend in verses 5 and on. This would usually be too mundane for me to notice, but I saw a light flicker.

Jesus is the bread of life. In John, when He speaks plainly about His metaphor of bread, He declares: "I am the bread of life" (John 6:35, 48).

His earthly life began in Bethlehem, a town whose name means "house of bread." Could it be that when He tells his disciples to ask for their daily bread He really means, "Daily, ask for Me." His words in the subsequent verses instruct the disciples to ask, seek, and knock that the Lord might give part of Himself in the Spirit.

The Lord daily provided bread from heaven (manna) in the desert, and He continues to provide daily bread. But the lesson to be learned from the provision in the desert should be the picture it gives us of daily sustenance. Let us see that such sustenance finds fulfillment in the person and presence of Jesus.

Why daily?

Why couldn't we have enough manna in the desert for tomorrow? What we receive in relationship today won't serve us tomorrow. The knowledge gained will lead us into deeper connection with the person, but knowledge and experience cannot substitute for presence.

Daily, we must depend. Daily we must ask and wait for the bread. And if we want to follow Jesus, we must depend on His presence; we must ask and wait for Him. I cannot have enough Jesus today to do without Him tomorrow.

I need Him every day.

Is this not the point of the gospel to be in God's presence through the reconciliation attained by His Son? To be fully in the presence of our fellow man through the reconciliation Jesus teaches?

Presence is the point.

It stood central in the garden at the beginning, and it stands central at the end of the story in being with God. What will we do now? We need bread daily. We need our friend every day. Ask for Him, seek Him, and knock on His door. He waits.

Adam

▢ **What is God providing for you today?**

▢ **What helps raise your awareness of God's presence, daily?**

▢ **What provision do you hold tightest, wanting to store up to be guaranteed for tomorrow?**

DAY 74

ENEMY TERRITORY

"Offense is 90% taken and 10% given."

— ANONYMOUS

| John 10:10 | 1 Peter 5:8 | 2 Corinthians 10:5-6 |

Along with much of the imagery in the book of Genesis, we put the devil in a storage closet to be sorted later, maybe when Halloween comes around. We can get behind the New Testament "neighbor" talk, and even loving the lepers, but the devil seems to be a poorly drawn cartoon character, an ill-willed, fast-food mascot that belongs with the Hamburglar and the like. Our college education interferes with belief in an evil tooth fairy.

It's impossible to witness the brokenness of the world, however, without ever wondering about its source. That realization often starts closer to home. Try as we might, we can't ignore our own brokenness. Even after becoming a follower of Jesus, our brokenness persists.

If God brings perfect peace, then why are we irate with the person who cut in front of us when a new cashier lane opens at

Whole Foods ? Why are we still offended at our mom's comment when we know she probably didn't mean it like that? Why are we jealous of our roommate when he or she gets extra days off work, and we must commute? I often find myself in darker, meaner places than I ever thought I'd be, seeing as I've already found the Hope of the world.

Sometimes spiritual warfare sounds like a scare tactic, a convenient way to thicken the plot of church daycare skits and services. Every good story needs a villain. But then who is the enemy when emotional reactions ruin our days and strain our relationships? Is it us?

Well, it's really a tag-team effort.

The enemy lobs the ball over home plate, and if we're not secure in Jesus, we're tempted to swing. When stressed or scattered, we make even easier targets. We take the bait, take offense and react angrily. Whether or not we see Him with a pitchfork and horns, we might see Him in our social anxiety. We might see Him in our impatience with and avoidance of others.

Jesus instructs us to take captive every thought. Keep our eye on the ball. This is not advice to be taken lightly when we realize what's at stake. The devil comes to steal, kill, and destroy our relationships. He comes to isolate.

Jesus wants us to be connected. The devil wants us to be divided. The more we become aware of the schemes the devil is using to steal our joy and wreck our relationships, the more (hopefully) prepared we'll be.

Hollis

———— ◆ ————

- To what extent do you struggle believing in the enemy?

- Why is the enemy's presence easier to forget than God's?

- What is the enemy's favorite tactic to trip you up?

DAY 75

BELIEF IN THE NOT-YET

"The answer must be, I think, that beauty and grace
are performed whether or not we will or sense them.
The least we can do is try to be there."

— ANNIE DILLARD

1 Corinthians 13:11-12	Romans 5:1-5	Matthew 14:22-27

Clarity arrives in reverse. The picture created by the puzzle materializes fully when the pieces configure in final combination. When scattered and strewn upon a table, the fractured picture is not a picture at all but instead a chaotic mess of meaningless shards. Although it carries the potential for something whole, in its uncompleted state, a puzzle remains something of the not yet.

Our lives at present often exist in this state. Scattered inside our hearts, inside our souls, are the loose pieces of singular hopes, dreams, relationships, experiences, and unfinished happenings. Often, we revert to discouragement, accepting the belief that these fragments will never fuse into a cohesive whole. We buy stock in the world's view of hopeless chaos and settle for the scattered show.

But something better must exist. The pieces must be part of a greater whole. Reconciliation of the apparent mess must be possible.

Someone once said that faith is seeing clearly in advance the things only understood in reverse, and Jesus lived this idea. He walked the earth with a focus on what existed beyond, living amid the fractured pieces yet assured of the completed picture that is a greater reality. People asked Him tangible questions, and He offered intangible answers. To the woman at the well, He offered living water. Baffled, she expected H_2O.

So what does it mean to live with this vision? How does it temper our interpretation of the world and the unreconciled nature of circumstantial happenings? If we could believe in the not yet, how would we read Scripture?

> Not only so, but we also glory in our sufferings, because we know that suffering produces perseverance; perseverance, character; and character, hope. And hope does not put us to shame, because God's love has poured out into our hearts through the Holy Spirit, who has been given to us. (Romans 5:3-5 NIV)

> Now faith is the assurance of things hoped for, the conviction of things not seen. (Hebrews 11:1)

> Do not let your heart be troubled; believe in God, believe also in Me. In My Father's house

are many dwelling places; if it were not so, I would have told you; for I go to prepare a place for you. If I go and prepare a place for you, I will come again and receive you to Myself, that where I am, there you may be also. And you know the way where I am going. (John 14:1-4)

Amy

——————•◆•——————

- What do you hope for in the not yet?

- How do you interact with God when you face discouragement?

- How does an awareness of the eternal inform you day to day?

THE SMALL THINGS

"All the small things."

— BLINK 182

Luke 19:11-27 | Matthew 25:14-30

In the 1990s, a prominent New York NBA player complained that the players in the league couldn't feed their families on the average NBA salary, which was $1 million a year in 1991. He couldn't feed his family on six zeros? Was his family a small nation?

Not every player retires broke after making millions of dollars a year in endorsements and salary. But somehow many do. Anyone think these guys should handle the federal budget?

The harsh reality looms: no one ever taught them how to handle even ten dollars. How do we expect them to manage a million dollars?

We need to teach our kids and ourselves how to handle a little. Learning to do so will teach us to handle much.

Social scientists say that if a man appears neat (i.e., tucked in shirt, lack of wrinkles, nice slacks and clean shoes) on a first date, the woman tends to think he will manage his life well. If he can take care of his appearance, he can probably take care of his house, his finances, and his marriage.

Henry Ford interviewed a young man to work for Ford Motor Company. The two went to a restaurant. When the entrees arrive, the young man added salt and pepper to his dish. Ford told him the interview was over; he said he can't hire people who make decisions about food without tasting it first. How could this man be trusted to make decisions about the nation's largest auto manufacturer if he couldn't make informed decisions with food?

To ever be faithful, to ever handle appropriately great quantities of anything, we must first prove ourselves capable of handling a few. We prefer governors to senators for the Oval Office because governors have governed a state; senators have not. We prefer coordinators to position coaches for head coaching jobs; they've managed an offense or defense.

Jesus makes this point bluntly. He instructs us to learn to manage our time, our gifts, our relationships, our money. How have we administered them?

Adam

————— ◆ —————

◻ Are Jesus' parables tributes to capitalism or something more?

◻ With what have you been entrusted to manage?

◻ How are you being faithful right now?

NOTHING IS MINE

"This world has nothing for me,
and this world has everything.
All that I could want and nothing that I need."

— CAEDMON'S CALL

| Luke 16:1-13 | Luke 17:7-10 | Matthew 20:1-16 |

This thought stays with me in my more enlightened moments: nothing is mine. To that end, or to move toward that end, I try to avoid saying something is mine. I try to say, "The car I drive" rather than "my car" or "the place I stay" rather than "my apartment." This comes easily since the computer I use belongs to my employer; the apartment belongs to the landlord, the car belongs to a bank, and the clothes I wear have mostly been given me. I don't even own my bed or desk.

In more enlightened moments, I try to think that everything in my possession belongs to God. And they do. The difficulty lies in remembering and acting accordingly.

If such items belong to God, I must treat them differently. I must care for them, but more importantly, I must think about how to use them. He's placed them in my custody, and one day He'll ask whether I used them well or wasted them.

This thought encompasses more than the material. We move from material to immaterial, perishable to eternal, visible to invisible. As I learn how to manage money, I begin to think how I can manage time. As I look at my use of time, I think about the use of my gifts. When I consider my gifts, I consider other gifts from the Lord: people. That's the direction of growth in Jesus' mind.

Will I faithfully care for the friend He's given me? Will I dutifully use my belongings to aid others, to serve them as He teaches? Will I offer my gifts back to Him in obedience to His purposes? Will I spend my days on me or on people and purposes larger than myself?

As I show myself capable of managing things, I can begin to manage time and gifts. Perhaps I'll grow into handling relationships well. The latter—things, time, and gifts—I need to see as tools to serve relationships. First, I serve the Lord and His agenda with these assets. Second, I serve the people around me. All are tools working to these ends. How will I use them? Whom will I serve?

Adam

- ▫ To what degree do you see your possessions as tools for a larger purpose or person?

- ▫ How have you used them? Give an example.

- ▫ What does it mean to be a steward of something? How is that worked out?

THE GREAT COMMISSION

DAY 78

ME FIRST

"The tribute to learning is teaching."

— WISE SAYING FROM THE ORIENTIS TEACHING

| Hebrews 5: 11-14 | Matthew 9:35-38 | 2 Timothy 2:1-7 |

Arrested development. This prison contains our spiritual lives and stifles our usefulness to God. Most of us squander our lives in this stagnant condition, rather than facing the uncomfortable thought of growth and challenge. Our laziness hurts the mission.

Jesus promises to make us "fishers of men." He wants us to be about the business of disciple making. Yet Paul's later admonition to the Hebrews resonates in us: "In fact, though by this time you ought to be teachers, you need someone to teach you the elementary truths of God's word all over again. You need milk, not solid food!" (Hebrews 5:12 NIV).

To effectively disciple others, we first must disciple ourselves. Do we pray? Are we connected to the true vine? Do we meditate on the truths of the Scriptures? Are we walking through life with a few friends who encourage, challenge, rebuke, and love us?

Discipleship, you see, is much about the art of imitation. The scores of younger men and women around us are looking for something true, authentic, and attractive. They imitate it. Then they embrace it. Soon you have a disciple.

At eighteen months old, my son Jeremy was already perfecting the art of imitation. One day, as my wife and I drove down the road, another car cut in front of us. "You jerk!" came the rebuke from the car seat in the back. Ouch. I guess he had heard that reaction a few too many times.

When Jesus said that the fields were white for the harvest (John 4:35), He was right. He still is today. There is no shortage of people who want to learn about life. The harvest doesn't lack. The harvesting crew does. Jesus urges us to pray for laborers.

I am part of a team that works with young people. The walk-in business is staggering. We need laborers. We need people who can teach. We need people who themselves are mature enough to pass along Jesus' principles to faithful men and women.

Will you make disciples? If so, you must first be a disciple. Few things will cause more growth. You see, teaching others is the best way for us to learn.

Brad

- ☐ Are you digesting spiritual milk or meat?

- ☐ How capable are you to teach from the Scriptures?

- ☐ How willing are you to invest in others through discipleship?

TEACH WHAT?

"Gettysburg. Fifty thousand men died right here on this field, fighting the same fight that we are still fighting among ourselves today. This green field right here, painted red. ... Listen to their souls, men. I killed my brother with malice in my heart. Hatred destroyed my family. You listen, and you take a lesson from the dead."

— COACH BOONE, REMEMBER THE TITANS

| Matthew 28:16-20 | John 13:33-35 | John 6:28-29 |

Antoine St. d'Exupery said, "If anything at all, perfection is achieved not when there is no longer anything left to add, but when there is nothing left to strip away."

So goes much thinking in business: do one thing and do it well. In education, teachers find that focusing on one concept a day will benefit students.

Simple works. Simple allows us to understand. Thus, some of us find simplicity a great help in approaching Scripture. Is its message one that is so simple? Does it come down to God's love and reconciliation?

Many of us cling to these texts. We believe that in them we find God's truth about who we are and how to live. But what is that message?

Jesus said to make disciples of all nations. He said to teach them all that He commanded.

What, then, did He command them? What did He teach?

I don't know about dispensational doctrine, reformed theology, systematic theology, or antinomianism. What it means to be Anabaptist, paleo-orthodox, Arminian or restorationist is lost on me. Thomism? Four- versus five-point Calvinism? Free will versus predestination? Ecumenical versus emergent? These have some value, but will we discuss these endlessly without thinking long and deeply about what Jesus said?

What He said sounds simple. He said the work of God is to believe in the one God sent. He said to be a follower of His, you must deny yourself, pick up your cross, and follow Him. He said the greatest commandment was to love God with everything in us. He said the second was like it, and that was to love our neighbor as we love ourselves.

All the Scriptures that came before, He said, hung on these two ideas: love God and love others, even our enemies. He said God does this. He did it. And His students Peter, John, James, and Paul all emphasized these ideas of forgiveness, grace, and reconciliation.

Could it be so simple? Love and believe? Follow Him? We can and will no doubt spend a great deal of time, maybe too much, debating particulars and parsing words. But this is what

Jesus said. This represents the teaching of Jesus, and this is what He tells us to teach others.

———•———

- ▢ **When you read the gospels, what strikes you as the focus of Jesus' words?**

- ▢ **What did Jesus communicate about Himself?**

- ▢ **What did Jesus communicate about God? How complex was it?**

HOW?

| Matthew 28:16-20 | Deuteronomy 6 | Mark 1:14-45 |

What does it mean to be intentional about making disciples? And why is this so important?

Jesus decided to interject Himself into human history at a certain time and into a certain tradition: Israel's rabbi culture during the Roman occupation. He could have chosen any time, any civilization, with any tool necessary.

Why not twenty-first century America? After all, the United States spreads its long shadow around the world. It exports billions of dollars in entertainment. And who wouldn't tune into Jesus on late-night TV?

Yet Jesus chose a minor occupied state during a relatively insignificant period of history. Why?

Rabbis walked the country with their disciples during Jesus' time. If you were one of the fortunate chosen few, the best of the best, the smartest of the smart, you might be asked by a rabbi to be his disciple. "Follow me" was the simple but profound invitation from a rabbi to live life under his instruction.

Then the dozen or so disciples would literally follow the rabbi. He would teach, much as God outlined in the Old

Testament: "These commandments that I give you today are to be on your hearts. Impress them on your children. Talk about them when you sit at home and when you walk along the road, when you lie down and when you get up. Tie them as symbols on your hands and bind them on your foreheads. Write them on the doorframes of your houses and on your gates" (Deuteronomy 6:6-9 NIV).

As each disciple followed his rabbi, the teacher would explain from the Scriptures as they encountered the many experiences of life. Each disciple had already memorized the entirety of the Hebrew Scripture, but each day brought a deeper understanding of the dynamic combination of truth and life. Rabbis used the most complete, interactive, three-dimensional, multi-media classroom known to man: the world around them. (Our educational system could learn a thing or two here.)

Jesus invested Himself and His twelve disciples into this culture. He rejected political power, fame, wealth, and influence during the three years with His followers. Then He handed the baton to them. Everything He had worked for was placed squarely into their hands:

> All authority in heaven and on earth has been given to me. Therefore go and make disciples of all nations, baptizing them in the name of the Father and of the Son and of the Holy Spirit, and teaching them to obey everything I have commanded you. And surely I am with you always, to the very end of the age. (Matthew 28:18-20 NIV)

Millions have followed Jesus through the ages because of these twelve. Strings of disciples passed His thoughts on through the ages.

To us.

Can we be as intentional about passing Jesus' thoughts to younger men and women? Will we teach them as we pass through life? Do we value this method as Jesus did? If so, who are you discipling right now? If not, who will you disciple?

Jesus wisely invested His life in discipleship. He wants us to do the same, to become "fishers of men."

Brad

———————◆———————

☐ **Describe discipleship in your own words. Does it work?**

☐ **What are you doing to become a disciple? To disciple others?**

☐ **Do you believe in this system as much as Jesus did?**

RACA

"The first problem for all of us, men and women,
is not to learn, but to unlearn."

— GLORIA STEINEM

| Matthew 5:22 | Matthew 7:1-5 | 1 Corinthians 3:18-23 |

Once on a fall night, I attended a concert. The performer was a singer-songwriter whose music I listen to practically every day. Although his work leans secular, I shared with a friend my suspicions about this musician's knowledge of Jesus.

My friend's look said, "Do you know anything at all? Have you heard his songs about booze and women and drugs? Do you know what Jesus said?" I just smiled. The exchange brought me back to Jesus' words in Matthew 5:22.

Why did He say, "whoever says, 'You fool,' shall be guilty enough to go into the fiery hell."? The commentators on this text always appeared to dodge something. Jesus' words cut a deep line in the dirt, but He wasn't just speaking against anger here, as scholars argue. He was talking about hell.

A friend, discussing this passage, helped illuminate what looked so cloudy to me. "A fool," he said, "was used for a person who did not know God." In Psalm 14:1 we read, "The fool has said in his heart, 'There is no God.'"

Are we calling people fools when we say they're not in the club? Are we in danger of hell when we say someone does or does not know God?

My friend then mentioned Jesus' comments about all power to judge being given to Him. Do we believe Jesus about this? If so, why do we claim authority to judge and then say, "This person can't possibly know anything about faith and Jesus"? Jesus' words on judgment in Matthew 7 are just as harsh as His words on calling people fools.

When we try to draw circles around people, saying, "You, you're in. And you, you're out," we sit in the place of God. We try to be God, assuming rights reserved only for Him. Didn't this lead to some problems in the garden? Will we ever learn about this attempt to be God?

A man wanted to know how many would be saved. Jesus responded, "Strive to enter through the narrow door" (Luke 13:24). When the disciples didn't approve of different followers, Jesus said, "He who is not against you is for you" (Luke 9:50).

When John wanted to call down fire on those who rejected Jesus, He said, I "did not come to destroy men's lives, but to save them." (Luke 9:56). "You don't get it," He says to us when we seek to define who is in and who is out.

He says to us, "You have nothing to say on this subject. It is not your territory. I will handle it. So be quiet. Do what I command and don't concern yourself with who is in and who is out, unless the person you're worried about is you."

Amy

———————— ◆ ————————

- ☐ **How do you sit in judgment and on whom?**
- ☐ **Why do we do this?**
- ☐ **Why does Jesus tell us to avoid doing this?**

THE BEST STUDENTS

"You cannot learn what you think you already know."

— EPICTETUS

| Luke 11:38-42 | Luke 9:46-48 | Luke 7:36-50 |

During Jesus' life and teaching, one group refused to listen. They were those who believed they already had all the answers. They were the religious elite. They had no time for Jesus because they had already solved life's mysteries and refused to ask further questions.

On the other hand, the social outcasts, tax collectors, followers of other religions, adulterers, drinkers, poor, crippled, children, these people understood. They could hear Jesus' teaching because they knew they didn't have answers tucked neatly into their back pockets. Whether it was their lack of knowledge, lack of acceptance by the world, or bodily failings, something led them to acknowledge a deficiency in themselves. They recognized the space He said He could fill.

For those who deny such a place exists, Jesus' words are deflected away. For those of us who deny this still, Jesus finds no audience, as He appears irrelevant and extraneous.

Steve Chalke recounts in his book *The Lost Message of Jesus* the story of British journalist John Diamond. Diamond wrote a weekly column for *The Times*, and in it he spoke openly of his struggle with throat cancer.

Many concerned people of faith wrote to the openly agnostic Diamond to urge his repentance and conversion, warning of the dangers of hell. This continued for a while, only making the skeptic increasingly skeptical of faith and its adherents. Finally, however, a Jesus follower and a cancer survivor wrote to Diamond asking if they could talk. He wanted to learn how Diamond was coping with cancer and to find out what he could learn from Diamond.

The journalist responded with these words: "The problem I have with Christians is they are so often the peddlers of certainty. You are the only Christian in the entirety of my life who has ever told me that they thought they could learn something from me. I'd love to meet you and talk further." John Diamond never made the meeting. He died the week after the column containing his reply was published.

We often specialize in processed answers that we carry anywhere, like ready-to-eat meals. We have what we need, or so we think, and because of that, we don't listen to others or the Lord to learn something new. We become like the religious elite of Jesus' day. Just as Jesus could perform no miracles in His hometown because the people lacked faith, so we can see nothing new of God. Our self-constructed box enclosing God keeps Him from acting outside its boundaries. We declare what He can do, with whom, and how (Matthew 15:9).

This is a tragedy.

We don't let Him teach us because we already have the answers. We don't allow ourselves to learn because we think we already know. We take short cuts to the end and miss the point of everything.

Adam

———◆———

- ❑ **What areas of brokenness in your life are you willing to admit?**
- ❑ **To what extent do you think you need love?**
- ❑ **How willing are you to be taught?**

DAY 83

THE FAITH OF JESUS

"Have you ever noticed the way Jesus
chose his disciples? From our vantage point,
it appears haphazard. Jesus walked along,
saw a guy fishing, and said, "Hey! You! Come with me,
and I'll unfold the greatest mysteries of the universe."

— BRIAN ANDREAS

| Luke 4:42-43 | Luke 5:29-32 | Matthew 26:31-35 |

When we dig deeper into the cultural context, we realize Jesus' nonchalance could be even more dire. The twelve He chose had most likely been rejected by the rabbis under whom they wished to study. They failed to meet the requirements. Rejected by the religious-cultural-social elite, most settled for the trades of their fathers.

Jesus likely chose twelve denied applicants. He prayed about them for a night (Luke 6:12-13) and then He probably said, "You are the ones I want. You will carry my message to the world, and you will change the world."

What?! Why didn't he check with HR? He could've seen that these guys didn't cut it. Sometimes people look great on paper but don't make the team. Sometimes they're great on paper, but they only make junior varsity. These guys looked awful on paper, and they became the starters.

What did they give in response? After living and walking with Him every day for three years, they bolted when the authorities came with a warrant.

He could have known this if He had looked more closely at their qualifications. They wanted to call fire down on people (Luke 9:51-56). They missed the points He taught (Matthew 16:1-11). They told Jesus to avoid death (Matthew 16:21-23), thinking He sought a political position. They even fought for first place in the kingdom (Matthew 20:20-28). These guys who walked and talked with Jesus every day regularly failed during the grading period and then bombed the final exam at His arrest.

What did Jesus have in mind?

One of them betrayed him. Ten others died cruel deaths. Yet those ten, and John, forever changed the world we know. Nothing has been the same since they walked the earth with Jesus. The world was permanently altered by the way they carried His message.

Despite their failures and setbacks and immaturity, Jesus continued to work in them. He didn't give up on them, even when they gave up on Him. These failures, these boys, were His workmanship, and He knew what they would do.

Jesus doesn't quit on His students. It may take them years, but they grow because of the faith their teacher has in them. He takes nobodies and makes them all stars—because of who He is. Because we're more than we know or believe ourselves to be in Him.

That's the faith of Jesus.

Adam

———◆———

- ☐ **What do you make of Jesus' selection of disciples?**
- ☐ **Who would you have chosen to change the world?**
- ☐ **Why do you think Jesus chose them?**

DAY 84

WHERE I AM RIGHT NOW

"For a long time it had seemed to me that life was about
to begin—real life. But there was always some obstacle
in the way. Something to be got through first,
some unfinished business, time still to be served,
a debt to be paid. Then life would begin.
At last, it dawned on me
that these obstacles
were my life."

— FR. ALFRED D'SOUZA

| Luke 9:57-62 | Mark 1:14-20 | Matthew 28:16-20 |

I don't love sermons about the Great Commission. I cringe, and something inside me rejects the guilt trip that pastors lay on parishioners. "Go into all the world and preach the gospel." They present this like a new idea or an old one that they just discovered.

Here we are performing our important church duties when aha! We forgot that we must be going into all the world to fulfill this command. We hear the sermon, and our minds start constructing a to-do list. Does a short-term missions trip suffice? What about my stint in the inner city? Could I schedule a visit to orphans in Zimbabwe next summer?

But why would Jesus command us to do something that nullifies our lives at present? Why must we *go* somewhere beyond our community to fulfill the Great Commission? Can we instead *go* into our own town?

The phrase should be translated "as you go." As we live our lives, we testify Christ.

But this is harder. My world at present is not ideal and certainly not lovable. I would rather sprinkle love on a two-week mission trip to Africa while my eyes still see that world as adventurous and romantic. I would rather love quickly when I am tangibly loved back with hugs and squeals of excitement from village children.

But then, what if Africa became my every day, perhaps then America would seem ideal? Or Asia, Australia or some other distant place? I could waste my entire life dreaming of far-off places to fulfill Jesus' command. It is far easier to see the Great Commission as something on which to embark in the future, rather than something we choose to live every day. It's easier to regard "God's will" for my life as something enigmatic and elusive rather than seeing it for what it is: what I am doing, here, now, in the present.

God does not want me to strive, molding myself into some contrived version of a model missionary. This is not fulfilling the command and following Him. He wants me to arrive at a place that is me, just more fully. He wants me to use my gifts, exercise my strengths, and live my life with a higher vision and purpose. God called the disciples from their professions as fishermen, not to transform them into astronauts but to make them better fishermen as they fished for men. He used tentmakers, carpenters, tax collectors, and even prostitutes.

We can go to Kenya and fulfill the Great Commission. We could go to the Starbuck's around the corner. We could go into our back yard or our kitchen. These are our worlds, and we must live in them fully, with our eyes open, our minds engaged, and our hearts ready.

What will we see as we go?

Amy

———•———

□ **What do you think the Great Commission includes?**

□ **What does it mean for you?**

□ **How would it be different in your life if Jesus' words really meant "As you go"?**

TAKES ONE TO MAKE ONE

"And in the end, I realized I received more than I gave."

— JOHN RUSKIN

| Hebrews 5:11-14 | 2 Corinthians 13:5-6 | James 1:19-25 |

I once played on a talented sports team that was thwarted by little coaching and less heart. One of the team's self-appointed leaders often complained about the coach.

"He's never played football. How can he teach us anything? I won't try to teach someone the violin if I've never played it. He's supposed to teach us about this game?"

His analysis, though logically flawed, held some truth. The teacher must first have knowledge to effectively impart it. A great football coach need not have played the game, but he must possess at least a minimal understanding of it.

Jesus said, "Make disciples of all the nations." He said we should pass his teachings to all the world. This admonition assumes that we've learned it first. That assumption, though fundamental to instruction, often gets brushed aside in the race to teach others. We forget to teach ourselves. Continually.

The best teachers always remained students. Their posture of learning gave them a greater understanding of learners. Their quest for greater insight carried them along new paths where they could then guide others.

Those hoping to instruct others in the ways of Jesus should take heed. How can we teach anyone Jesus' commands if we ourselves won't or don't know them from experience? Can we speak of the consequences, good and bad, of such obedience? Can we speak of and sympathize with the cost of such choices? Can we tell others of the great rewards and new understandings that come from hearing and doing Jesus' teachings?

If we plan to teach others what Jesus has taught us, we need to have been taught. To make disciples of Jesus' teachings, we must have learned them. John Stuart Mill, in one of his attacks on faith in Jesus, said, "If it were true, I suppose I would've seen it at least attempted."

Do you attempt it? Or do you simply tell others about it?

---◆---

- ☐ **Do you teach others about Jesus based on experience or only what you've read?**

- ☐ **How do you remain a student of Jesus?**

- ☐ **Do you place emphasis on "knowing enough" material or on hearing and obeying Jesus' teachings?**

LOOK BEFORE YOU LEAVE

"To labor is to pray."

— MOTTO OF THE BENEDICTINES

| Matthew 9:35-10:20 | Luke 10:1-20 | John 4:31-38 |

Before Jesus sent the disciples to teach others, He told them to do one thing.

After Jesus mentioned the need for workers, he said the first thing they should do is pray.

He didn't tell these boys to rush off. He told them to pray before He gave them a few instructions. He didn't suggest a few reading materials, though they had probably memorized the entire Hebrew Bible. He didn't tell them about some classes they needed to take, and He didn't give them pamphlets. These guys went without a map, statistics on demographics, or any great deal of experience.

Jesus put His message in the hands of horribly unqualified people. What sort of operation did He think He could run? Just pray? What did He think that would do?

He communicated the message that one thing mattered. These guys needed to depend on God. Not very macho or efficient, no, but He never claimed to run a Fortune 100 company either. He simply wanted His followers to ask God to do the work. He didn't display much concern with their qualifications or titles.

But another thing: if these teachings of Jesus carried healing to sick people and life to the dying, why did He not encourage them to hurry it up? Why dawdle with prayer? If the disciples have the goods, why delay?

Perhaps Jesus wanted them to remember whose business they represented. These twelve guys did not draft this agenda, and they alone would not accept responsibility for its success or failure. When Jesus talks about a harvest, He refers to the Lord of the harvest.

"Listen up, fellas. We'll go over this one more time. Whose business is this?"

"The Lord's."

"And who is in charge here? Who calls the shots, gets the glory, and does the work?"

"The Lord."

"Okay. Now pray that you don't forget it, thinking this is about you and how clever you are. Ask the One in charge. He'll take care of things."

I wonder if this would fly today. Would any relief organization looking to heal disease or combat sickness approach their work like this? Would any religious group or organization? Probably few. But maybe that's because they go about their business their way and God goes about His business His way.

Adam

———————◆———————

□   **When you see need in the world, what is your first response?**

□   **Why would Jesus tell the disciples to pray first?**

□   **How willing are you to wait on God before you do what you think He wants done?**

WHOSE?

"Come together, right now, over me."

— THE BEATLES, "COME TOGETHER"

| 1 Corinthians 3:1-9 | Luke 9:46-50 | John 17:20-26 |

The movie *Remember the Titans* contains a scene that elicits laughs while illustrating a point.

Herman Boone is the newly hired black football coach at T. C. Williams High School in Alexandria, Virginia, during the racially tense seventies. Before he takes his new and racially mixed team to camp before the season, he has a small exchange with his all-American linebacker, Gary.

"Once you step on that bus you, ain't got your mama no more. You got your brothers on the team, and you got your daddy. Gary, if you want to play on this football team, you answer me when I ask you who is your daddy. Who's your daddy, Gary?"

"You."

"And whose team is this, Gary? Is this your team? Or is this your daddy's team?"

"Yours."

Boone faced the unenviable task of building a team comprised of players at considerable enmity with one another. Skin, background, and a slew of prejudices divided them.

Does Jesus not face the same issues with us? Could He not have a similar conversation with each of us?

"You have no organization. You have your brothers and sisters. And who is your teacher? Who's your leader?"

Jesus might then ask, "And whose plan is it? Whose world is it? Is it yours, or is it mine? Is it your good news, or is it mine? Do you have the trademark to this good news? Do you lead me? Or does the message instruct you? Do I lead you? Whose teachings are these? Whose team are you on?"

Sadly, we need to confront these questions. We receive the charge of loving our brothers and working with them as we work with Jesus, and we immediately divide. Bureaucracy and office politics rule the day. Like fiery and territorial John, we say, "Those folks can't work for Jesus because they don't follow with us. Let's shut 'em down. They don't do this right, they say that wrong, and they're too fluffy or stodgy."

And still He asks, "Whose team is this? Whose plan is this?"

He leads. We follow. We co-labor with Him. If we want others to look at Jesus as a leader, teacher, and someone worthy of listening to, we should listen to Him ourselves.

"Come together. Right now. Over me."

Adam

- Do you think more about Jesus' agenda or yours?

- What is His agenda?

- How do you carry it out?

METHODS AND NUMBERS? OR PRESENCE AND INDIVIDUALS

"One love, one life ... we get to share it."

— U2, "ONE"

| 1 Corinthians 2:1-5 | Matthew 28:20 | Matthew 18:19-20 |

"That's a trap!" he said. "That's a sneaky, manipulative trap."

Arguing with my buddy on an issue of morality, I caught him in a logical fallacy. I pounced on it and forced him to choose between two options he detested.

He was right. I think logic has lost its place in our debates, and we should lament its passing. But am I going to venerate logic to the detriment of a friendship with my buddy? I have no doubt that he'd respond more to the latter than the former. Do I care more about him or about proving a point? I can care for him *and* about the point without needing to hit him over the head with it.

To what does someone respond more: techniques or personality? Do we want them responding to Jesus or to our Wharton School and Carnegie marketing campaigns?

While I talk about Jesus, do I think about Him and His extravagant love or about how to persuade the other?

Let's not create a straw man out of talking about Jesus. But remember that we often think more about technique than we do about His personhood. Only the latter can change my heart. Only the latter can speak to someone else's.

Should we then not ask whether we depend upon Jesus' presence or upon learned techniques? If we lean toward techniques, do they have anything to do with Jesus? Do we memorize a litany of questions, or do we care for each individual as an individual, as someone worthy as an end in themselves? Do we recognize the vast and incalculable worth of each person?

Jesus taught that a shepherd would leave ninety-nine sheep to find one. The one is that valuable. He told us about a woman with ten coins searching for the one that was lost. We focus on reaching many rather than caring for one. Could it be that caring for just one most fully illustrates Jesus' message? Jesus wanted the presence of the one.

Too often, we leave one for the ninety-nine. He's trying to reach us. He's reaching out for me. I am the one. He's trying to meet us that we might walk together. Maybe when we meet, we'll introduce others to him and forget about proving our next point.

Would Jesus have been a very good evangelist by this standard of reaching more?

Adam

————◆————

- ▢ **To what degree should we use sales techniques when we talk about Jesus?**

- ▢ **To what degree did Jesus use sales techniques in dealing with people?**

- ▢ **To what degree do you view people like Jesus did—and still does?**

NATURAL ATTRACTION

"If you build it, they will come."

— FIELD OF DREAMS

| Acts 2 | Acts 4 | John 17 |

No one looks at a feuding couple and says, "I want that!" No one thinks, *I can't wait to have a distant and dead marriage where both of us live on opposite ends of the house and rarely speak.* The same holds true for friends or teams or groups that treat one another coldly. It's just not a pretty sight.

People do see couples that love each other and say, "I want what they have."

People see organizations where individuals are valued and celebrated, and say, "I want to work there." This happens innately. When people come together to love one another, others are drawn to them.

No marketing degree from Berkley or Chicago is needed to understand this attraction. You want a business ranked in the top 100 companies for whom to work? Care about the employees. Look at Fortune's top ten companies for which to work. They each do something exceptional to show employees they are valued.

Do you want your children to have a successful marriage? Stand and model such a relationship yourself. Chances are their vision for marriage will come from what they see their parents do.

Do you want people to want what you teach? Do you want to "add to your numbers" or "reach more"? Love those around you, and others will come. If you gauge your success by numbers because of your capitalist upbringing, question this. Maybe you need to attract only one. You can't talk deeply with a thousand anyway.

If you fancy yourself a teacher, you need students. The best students, however, turn out to be those who seek out their teacher. They want to learn. Chase those who you think need to learn, and you'll find hard heads and deaf ears. Find one who has approached you, and you have someone who's ready to learn, to grow. The question is how you find one.

Again, we return to love. To find the one, love the co-worker in your office, the wife of your youth, or the friend from high school. Others will come.

If you're in the church business, this principle holds. Jesus said it long before *Field of Dreams*. Jesus exclaimed the "if you build it, they will come" sentiment long ago : "By this everyone will know you are My disciples, if you have love one for another" (John 13:35). Then "they may be brought to complete unity.

Then the whole world will know that you sent me and loved them, even as you have loved me" (John 17:23 NIV).

If you love, others will come to you.

Adam

———— ◆ ————

◻   **Are you trying to reach others from something? What? And why?**

◻   **How do you try to reach others?**

◻   **What specific ways do you want to make your cause magnetic?**

DISCIPLESHIP FOR DUMMIES

"Jesus tapped me on the shoulder and said,
'Bob, why are you resisting me?'
I said, 'I'm not resisting you!'
He said, 'You gonna follow me?'
I said, 'I've never thought of that before."

— BOB DYLAN

| Luke 9:57-62 | John 14:1-7 | Matthew 16:24-27 |

Jesus gave the disciples a grand commission. Long discussions and numerous conferences focus on Matthew 28:19-20. We could discuss this at length and analyze the various aspects, but let's look at one element of the commission.

Who are the disciples? If I am one or want to be a student of this Jewish teacher, how do I become one?

Perhaps we might say that following Jesus carries a couple of key elements. Some will say this is too reductive, and others will say this is too complicated, and others will say I've missed nothing but the main point.

First, we learn from Him. We listen to what He says. We learn from Him and try to do what He says. And He asks a lot: "Deny yourself." "Take up your cross." "Follow me." In effect, He says, "Lose your agenda. Know that this whole affair costs more than anything you could imagine. And follow where I lead."

Second, while listening, trying to learn and obey, we must believe Him. Believe what? The things He says about Himself, about God, about us. This proves to be a challenge.

Learning from Him, we ponder what Jesus said. His words make sense because doing what He says means forsaking our own agenda. It is costly, and it does lead to being sent out.

"Go! Proclaim the kingdom ... heal ... baptize ... teach them to obey all that I commanded you." He says these things. He tells us to do them.

We do it because He tells us to. What happens in the carrying out of this grand task of teaching others the secrets He's whispered in our ears? We learn them. They develop into something real. Like the toys in Geppetto's woodshop, those of us doing and obeying start feeling as if we are coming to life. We are learning life from its great teacher.

We become His students as we believe and do what He says. We are disciples as we approach Him, giving up what we have sought for ourselves to believe and carrying out what He seeks to give this world.

Adam

———◆———

- ☐ **What is your definition of discipleship? How have you carried this out?**

- ☐ **What needs to change?**

- ☐ **What do you do in following Jesus that makes others follow Him as well?**

"When reading *The Voices of the River*, I cannot help but think of connections. As I live through his own early-life exposure to rivers, bird sound and fish, I think of my own explorations through the Black Hills as a youth. His later-in-life journeys through the watersheds of Montana, Alaska, and Maine are made through his deep connection to certain species of trout. In doing so, he shows how he has developed a connection to the natural world around him in a way that challenges us to find our own. Not only so that we may be reunited in some way with the natural world, but to see how our behavior as a human species—our often short-sided behavior through development and efforts to 'tame' nature—deeply endangers an entire chain of life that ultimately affects us. From creating imbalance to rivers and fish or altering the natural relationship between predator and prey, we have caused imbalance, lost our connections. Matthew's words help us to realize this, invite us into a world where we are aware and in balance, and give us hope."

  –CARL JOHNSON, award-winning Alaskan photographer, author of *Where Water is Gold: Life and Livelihood in Alaska's Bristol Bay*

"Dickerson's reflections in *The Voices of Rivers* alert readers to the primal beauty and strength of waters wild or tame, and their inhabitants, from trout and beaver, to loon and snipe and harlequin duck. The music of the elements and the shaping of wild landscape and water-scape hold for him reminders of the rhythms of the earth, both rugged and fragile before the onslaught of the human animal and his depredations."

  –LUCI SHAW, Writer in Residence, Regent College, author *Thumbprint in the Clay*

"*The Voices of Rivers* reveals one man's passion for the natural world with stories of the biology, ecology, and the conservation of rivers and the wild life dependent on them. Weaving the writings of naturalists and scientists with his experiences with biologists and conservationists in dozens of waterways from across North America, Dickerson shares his passion and feelings towards our shared responsibility to protect everything associated with them. The reader becomes part of the excitement of the cast, the splendor of the views from a rivers bank, and learns that if one slows their experience to that of the water they too will hear the voices of rivers."

  –BRUCE CONNERY, Biologist

"Dickerson channels Wendell Berry, almost as if Berry were a mentor; and even if he's not named, Thoreau finds a way in to these lovely wilderness forays. All the way through *The Voices of Rivers*, the author wields his fly rod as elegantly as he does his pen, and the result is more than a wilderness sojourn— it's a pilgrimage."

—JAMES CALVIN SCHAAP, author of *Touches the Sky*

"I learned from *The Voices of Rivers* about the Welsh concept of 'hiraeth.' Dickerson describes it as 'the powerful sense of longing for something good and beautiful.' Hiraeth bleeds through Dickerson's book. Whether in the search for native cutthroat through the writing of Wendell Berry in Glacier National Park; or the quest for Dolly Varden in Alaska, this book is a breath of fresh air. Read it to learn about the solace and beauty of fishing for wild trout and salmon. Read it to learn about how we can re-knit our lands and waters. Read it to better comprehend the greed and selfishness of those that would despoil landscapes such as Bristol Bay, Alaska. Read it."

—CHRIS WOOD, President and CEO, Trout Unlimited

"If Izaak Walton's *Compleat Angler* deserves credit for inspiring the rich literature of fly-fishing, Matthew Dickerson's *The Voices of Rivers* immediately merits a place at the current end of that enticing shelf. In addition to Dickerson's vivid accounts of fishing for trout (mostly) in the rivers of Colorado, Montana, Alaska, and Maine, his new book also conveys a thoughtful and informative perspective on trout ecology and conservation and the importance of public lands for the health of our earth. His highly engaging voice ties this all together with its narrative energy, excitement, and humor. Dickerson's approach to fishing is in most cases catch-and-release. But this book is definitely a keeper."

—JOHN ELDER, author of *Reading the Mountains of Home*

"*The Voices of Rivers* accords readers with a bird's eye view of fly fishing for wild trout and salmon in some of America's most beautifully intact ecosystems from Maine to Montana to Alaska. The author gives a prolonged shout-out to federal and state public lands for their recreational and environmental value for all Americans."

—JOHN BRANSON, Historian